T0356108

Praise for *All the Ways Our Dead Still Speak*

"*All the Ways Our Dead Still Speak* is a stunning book about death, life, faith, and the love that binds all of us to each other. The story Caleb Wilde weaves together feels, at times, like a near-death experience: a powerful, hopeful, and life-altering encounter with the other side."
—Matthew Paul Turner, #1 *New York Times*–bestselling author
of *What Is God Like?* and *When God Made You*

"There's a weird hush around afterlife connections—like if you're smart, you don't believe in these things. Caleb Wilde is one of the kindest, most intelligent, most articulate people I know, which means his new book, *All the Ways the Dead Still Speak*, will help peel away any shame or shyness you have around holding space for those you love."
—Megan Devine, author of *It's OK That You're Not OK*

"Caleb Wilde once again brings us into the funeral parlor of our hearts and lets us all weep. *All the Ways Our Dead Still Speak* is a delicious and intimate look at one man's process of dealing with death and how a slight shift in our understanding of death can bring peace and healing to an often dreaded experience. All of us can learn to grieve and reconnect with our beloved ancestral roots because of Wilde's words."
—Kevin Garcia, mystic theologian and practitioner,
and author of *Bad Theology Kills*

"I think for a long time we thought that when someone died, we were supposed to let go of them and move on. Caleb Wilde's *All the Ways Our Dead Still Speak* shows us all the reasons why the opposite is true. This deeply reassuring book is for anyone who has ever grieved deeply, wondered where their loved ones are, and yearned to stay connected to them."
—Claire Bidwell Smith, author of *Anxiety:*
The Missing Stage of Grief

"Having worked at a funeral home through college, then plying my pastoral trade in many a funeral home for nearly four decades, I found *All the Ways Our Dead Still Speak* speaking volumes. But don't be misled: what appears to be a book about death is actually a book about life and its deepest, most imperative questions. This gifted and perceptive writer peers into our souls, takes us down roads traveled and roads yet to be traveled, and brings us home."

—Philip Gulley, author of *If Grace Is True* and
the Harmony and Porch Talk series

"*All the Ways Our Dead Still Speak* is a deep, intentional exploration of lineage, ancestry, and the living, breathing influence and pervasiveness of the dead. In beautiful and exploratory writing, Caleb Wilde reminds us that the dead—and their legacies, stories, and wounds—do not live 'back there,' but 'up here,' alongside us each and every day."

—Shelby Forsythia, author of *Your Grief, Your Way*

"Caleb Wilde's stories of life, love, and death as a funeral director reveal all the ways the dead remain with us and remind us who we are. As I read, I allowed myself to feel closer to my own parents, whose spirits live in my writing but whose bodies have been transformed into soil on the land back home. This book reminded me that I will always carry their love and that their voices will carry me too."

—Mallory McDuff, author of *Our Last Best Act:
Planning for the End of Our Lives to Protect
the People and Places We Love*

All the Ways Our Dead Still Speak

All
the Ways
Our Dead
Still Speak

A Funeral Director on Life,

Death, and the Hereafter

CALEB WILDE

Broadleaf Books
Minneapolis

CONTENTS

PREFACE

Our family's funeral home has six generations and more than 170 years of established trust with the community of Parkesburg, Pennsylvania, and the surrounding area. It's rare that we don't personally know at least one member of each of the nearly three hundred families we serve each year. That generational trust has made me privy to some of my community's most vulnerable and sacred moments. Since most of my writing is inspired by those moments, my number-one rule is to protect those at the center of my work by making sure I obscure any identifying details.

I'd like to think that my first book, *Confessions of a Funeral Director*, has maintained its number-one spot on the Parkesburg Authors Best-Selling Books list because it's kept the trust—although I'm pretty sure it's the only book on the list. There are probably a few quiet critics of my first book in the Parkesburg community who thought it was poorly written or hated the fact that it included so much of my spiritual journey. But so far no one has pulled me aside and told me that my retelling and publishing of their story had caused them further pain.

In *Confessions of a Funeral Director*, I said that the stories in the book were like Frankenstein's monster: pieces of stories sewn and stitched together to create something all its own.

Like Frankenstein's monster and all the dead human parts that made him, the individual stories were less distinguishable, thus protecting the privacy of the families we serve while still having life in them.

As I was drafting *All the Ways the Dead Still Speak* and thinking about how to represent the many voices, perspectives, and experiences I've witnessed through my work at the funeral home, and how to honor the privacy of those in our community, I decided to employ the creative nonfiction device of the composite character. This craft choice allows a writer of nonfiction to Frankenstein not only the stories but the characters as well. I want to explain how I created and approached two composite characters, Gerda and Celeste.

Gerda and Celeste are the result of a multitude of voices I've listened to and a myriad of stories I've been told by those I serve at the funeral home. Instead of having different characters for each chapter and each story, this book gives Gerda and Celeste some story arc, which allows them to talk about and experience some of the stories I've heard and the things I've experienced. Gerda and Celeste simplify the experiences for you, the reader, while also protecting the privacy of those who have told me these stories.

Distilling these stories and characters into creative composites to help clarify my ideas and understanding is in the interest of the truth. It's the most truthful way I can write this book because there are so many voices, so many stories, so many perspectives that I've experienced over the years. Any attempt to focus on the factual accuracy of the multitude of stories—instead of the *truths* that come out of the stories— would only makes things less clear, less poignant, and less reflective of the relationship I've come to have with my own ancestors.

Chaplain Celeste is my attempt to embody the people at Mt. Zion African Methodist Episcopal (AME) Church, who have loved on me, inspired me, and pastored me simply by allowing me to serve them as a funeral director. I have the utmost respect for that church family, and I do the best I can to represent what I've learned through them in the character of Celeste. I need Celeste's voice in this book because I want you to know where many of the thoughts in this book about ancestors and afterlife came from. They didn't come from me, as a white man. Celeste's character claims ownership for ideas that weren't wrought by me or my white ancestors.

Gerda's conversation points are reflective of the many voices that have skeptical concerns about God, the afterlife, and ancestors. Her character touches on experiences I've been told about interactions and visions but from a critical standpoint. I'm both a person of faith and a skeptic, and Gerda reflects the skeptical part of my personal contradiction. Writing across race and culture and gender is a fraught enterprise, and in representing these composite characters, I am sure I have made mistakes. I welcome any critical feedback with an open mind and heart.

In addition, my story is rooted in my memory, and most of the conversations are paraphrased. Almost all the names of people in this book—except for my family—have also been changed and details obscured to protect people's privacy.

Having said all this, I want to emphasize that the afterlife-focused stories are based on real experiences. The facts about our family business and the story of our funeral home are also sourced from both written and oral memory. The story of the Christiana Resistance is sourced from three books on the subject noted in the back of the book. My conversations with my therapist are paraphrased and are summaries of approximately two years of therapy. My own stories are told as factually as I can tell them.

If you're from the Parkesburg community, you will likely recognize some of these stories. I want to assure you that I've done my best to honor your stories, including this craft decision to use composite characters. If I've failed in any way, I want you to know that it was not my intention. I love you all, and I hope this book gives voice to many of the things you've told me and my family over the years.

This is a book for those of you who—like me—want to reconnect with our deceased loved ones, make sense of the different experiences we may have had since their passing, and understand a more progressive view of the afterlife. If those are some of your goals, I hope my journey around the dead and dying can provide some insight. The afterlife is waiting to reconnect, and I'm hoping this book can provide a path to connection.

—

Writing this book has taken far more energy than it should have. It's not because there's a lack of talking points about ways the dead speak to us right now. I could share a lot of stories about both the dying and the living connecting with their dead. This book took a lot of energy because I wrote most of it during the pandemic while working long hours as a funeral director. The pandemic brought us a taxing 20 percent more death calls than the last five-year average. On top of the high volume, trying to guide grieving families during a pandemic felt all-consuming and, on a number of occasions, caused tough bouts with professional burnout.

Two months after my first book was published, in November 2017, I made a trip out to Los Angeles to record a podcast with Rob Bell in his backyard studio (the interview is episode 174 of the RobCast). During the interview, Rob prompted me to talk about stories I had heard about deathbed visions. I told him that about one-fourth of the families we serve have some kind of story to tell about the thin space between death and life.

Unknown to me at the time, a variety of reports on the prevalence of deathbed visions suggest something similar. One study that analyzed hospice patients reported 39 percent of 575 families interviewed claimed that their loved ones had a deathbed vision. In a nationwide Japanese survey, out of 2,221 families, 21 percent of the dying had seen deathbed visions, with most of those being visions of ancestors.

It's hard to define what constitutes a "deathbed vision," and that may be part of the reason that there's such a discrepancy between one study and the next. Generally, deathbed visions are seen as something other than a hallucination because the dying person who experiences deathbed visions is otherwise lucid and demonstrating mental clarity.

In the middle of the interview, Rob said, "Here's what I think would be interesting—not that you asked. I think the liminal space and what happens in the threshold where they're not alive and not dead: that's the book you should write. A lot of times an [afterlife] book is like, 'How to Prove There's Life After Death.' It becomes a proof. It's like a court trial: 'We're going to prove that something happens after you die.' To me, what's much more compelling is just stories. Because you don't have an agenda: 'I'm just telling you what happened. I'm just telling you what they told me. I'm just telling you what they saw.' I would read that book in a heartbeat."

Then, in January 2020, an editor at Broadleaf Books, Valerie, reached out to me to ask if I had any book proposals I was working on. I told her that I wanted to write a book that dances around a progressive view of the afterlife. Valerie wrote back, "Would you believe that I have a wish list of acquisitions, and a progressive view of the afterlife is on that list? Seriously."

By April 2020, the pandemic was in full swing. The workload at the funeral home was so intense that it really didn't make sense for me to go home, so I just decided to live at the funeral home. I stayed there until the first wave of COVID deaths had passed, but in the middle of my stay, I signed a book contract with Broadleaf. In the contract, I specifically asked that the deadlines for the book publication be held loosely because I had no idea how the pandemic would affect my personal and professional life.

It's difficult enough to write a book while you're working full time at a funeral home and have two young boys who need their daddy's love. But during a pandemic? Creativity and focus were so difficult for the first year. I'd start writing and then work would spike. I'd start writing again and then we had to create safety standards at the funeral home.

I'd start again and Jeremiah needed to be homeschooled, and Nicki and I had to pick up the slack. I'd start again and a few of my family members got COVID. I'd start again and I had to wrestle with how to run an incredibly busy business while some of the funeral home staff had COVID. You get the idea. It's hard to keep finding the energy to restart and restart and restart and restart a book.

As I was writing, it became more and more apparent that the message it contained was a message that could speak directly to those who lost a loved one during the pandemic, either from the coronavirus itself or other causes. The pandemic created isolation and loneliness that I'm sure we all felt. Parenting was lonely. Grief was especially lonely while the pandemic raged. People had funerals alone. People were actively dying alone. People died alone.

Except here's the thing: I don't think we're ever truly alone. Perhaps now more than ever, we need to hear stories about all the ways our dead still speak.

If anything, writing this book during the pandemic pushed me to continuously rekindle the creative spark that the virus kept putting out. My stop-and-start dance with death work blew past the draft deadlines by a few months. "I'm going keep being kind to myself" became a mantra. I'd restart again and again and again. After a year and a half worth of agains, here I am, at the end of the manuscript, and I know it didn't get the undivided attention it deserved. *Nothing* did during the pandemic. All of us felt pulled in so many different directions, fragmented into little pieces of ourselves.

Yet despite those misgivings, this book is a realized account of how my reconnection with my ancestors and the afterlife carried me through the pandemic. Although I never meant it to happen that way, this book found much of its material through my real-life struggles while working through the pandemic. Had I written this before the pandemic, the book would not have been nearly as personal and intimate as it is in present form.

The pandemic brought my life into focus, and it turns out that the only way I could move forward was with the empowerment of the voices of the dead. This book may not be the best writing that I've signed my name to, but I'm not sure anything during the pandemic felt whole and perfect. It is, however, a story that changed the trajectory of my life and the lives of my ancestors.

—Caleb Wilde

CHAPTER 1

A DREAM OF HEAVEN

I walked into Our Lady of Consolation Church carrying the church truck, the accordion-like collapsible cart that we use to hold the casket. I couldn't help but notice all the Advent pageantry. Red and white potted poinsettias checkered the chancel. In the rear of the church, a vintage nativity scene that had survived five or six generations of Parkesburg parishioners sat proudly, a yearly Advent fixture. The artificial evergreen Advent wreath had all four candles burning, while evergreens of the real variety snaked around the lit pew torches flanking the center aisle. Through the open door to the sacristy, I could see that Father Michael had the seasonally colored funeral pall laid on a chair, with his matching vestment hanging on an overburdened wire hanger. It was Christmas Eve, and I could smell the holiday and all the wonderful memories that accompany it.

As a funeral director, I find a certain freedom in working funerals in and around the holidays. There's a sense that I'm "volunteering" to work on a holiday (although that may just be a coping mechanism on my part). And families are more gracious with us, knowing that we're likely missing out on our own family events. This Christmas Eve funeral seemed particularly special because it was the funeral for a very dear friend of ours, Joan Ricci.

Joan had been the organist at Our Lady for the better part of a decade. Every time we had a funeral mass at the church—which was roughly fifteen times a year—she was there, with her warm smile and genuine love, playing the funeral mass hymns and harmonizing with the cantor.

Joan had the uncanny ability to communicate love with her presence. There was a sense of love so thick it could almost be seen and touched, and it spread. To everyone.

Joan also had breast cancer the entire time I knew her. A roller coaster of breast cancer. It would be in partial remission, and then it'd come back. At one point she was declared cancer free, but it came back again. She beat it one last time—her doctors thought it might be gone for good—until it came back with full vengeance. Joan was fifty-two when she died, leaving behind her husband and three teenage children.

After I entered the church, Pop-Pop was soon behind me, carrying a couple of flower basket stands. My grandfather, my dad's dad, had aged quickly over the past year. A year ago he had been meeting with families, working all the funerals, answering the business phone, all at the age of eighty-two.

If you read my previous book or know anything of my story, you know that both my mom and my dad came from funeral home families. I'm a sixth-generation funeral director on my dad's side, the Wildes. And my mom grew up in the Brown Funeral Home, in the neighboring borough of Christiana, where her father was the third-generation funeral director in his family. Since my mom now works as the secretary at the Wilde Funeral Home, I'm a fifth-generation deathcare worker on my mom's side. You could say death runs in every family, but it seems to have a special run in mine.

Following five generations of funeral directors on one side of my family and four on the other, I grew up thinking there wasn't any other real option. Looking back, I wasn't sure if I had ever been given the confidence to make my own decision.

"It's a good business, Caleb," Pop-Pop Brown would tell me. And he was right.

"This is a ministry, Caleb," was the mantra Pop-Pop Wilde would say. And he was right too.

Since both of my grandfathers came from funeral businesses that were generations deep, I doubt those narratives were theirs. I'm sure both of them were told the same things by their fathers, mothers, and grandparents. Families rarely build generational businesses without creating a mythical story.

Now, closing in on eighty-three, Pop-Pop Wilde still liked to occasionally embalm and dress the deceased, because he could take it at his own pace. But the rest of the funeral business was too tiring. Officially in heart failure, he found it exhausting just to make it up the stairs and into Our Lady's sanctuary.

Leaning against a pew, he looked at me said, "Don't get old, Calebee." He'd affectionately called me "Calebee" from time to time in years before, but now, as he grew more dependent on my help, it was all he called me.

"It's better than the other option," I shot back with a smile. Working in the funeral industry made us very aware of the "other option."

He pushed off the pew, started walking toward the chancel, and called back, "Some days I'm not so sure."

Pop-Pop had made funeral arrangements with the Ricci family because he loved Joan. He was here at her funeral because he wanted to be. This was the first funeral he had worked in over a month, and I wasn't sure he had the stamina for it. I had decided that I'd stick by his side the entire day, give him as many breaks as he was willing to take, and stand close to him when he was working in case he became faint.

Pop-Pop had talked to Father Michael over the phone a couple of days ago. They both expected Joan's funeral to be huge, and they wanted to make sure they were on the same logistical page.

I walked behind Pop-Pop, watching his slow, uneven gait, as he told me about the conversation he had with Father Michael, who he affectionately called, "Father Mick."

"Mick said that Joan's death was one of the most spiritual experiences he'd ever had," Pop-Pop said as we reached the front of the church. "He was there when she died. He told me he's been crying ever since."

Out of all the priests and pastors in the area, Pop-Pop got along with Father Mick the most, mainly because he could be his fun-loving self around Father Mick. Father was a quintessential Philadelphian. He knew how to have a good time, and becoming a priest hadn't changed that. In fact, it seemed that he, too, recognized that his Phillyness didn't always gel with the priesthood. He admits that he was surprised he was accepted into seminary and says he tried to quit six times before finally graduating. When he was ordained, he said he laid prone on the floor of the Cathedral of Saints Peter and

Paul, fearful he would not last in the priesthood. Two years away from retirement, Father was nearing the end of something he never thought would begin.

Father was one of the priests who never tried to be spiritual. Everyone knew he smoked. He didn't try to hide it. He'd curse on occasion, and people knew that too. He liked to drink. Nobody was too concerned about that either. He'd even allow non-Catholics like Pop-Pop and me to receive his blessing during the Eucharist. He had fallen into his spirituality, not sought it out. If you met him at a bar, you'd never know he was a priest—not because he was wild, but because you could see that his soul bore the same struggles as yours did.

In fact, the only people I ever heard Father criticize were the ones that were overbearingly religious. When he first came to Our Lady, a number of the uptight parishioners left in favor of stricter pastures. Honestly, it made the church better. The people who stayed didn't wear their religious logos on their shirts like the ones who left. The people who stayed were the kind who just wore plain old shirts, most of which had blue collars and a barbecue stain here or there.

Joan was the same. She didn't wear her faith logo loud and proud. She never talked about her cancer, unless you asked her how she was doing. None of us would have even known if it hadn't been for her closest friends feeding us updates. Which is why the last time the cancer came back, I, like most people in town, didn't even know. When we received the death call from Joan's hospice nurse, we responded with disbelief. We'd just seen her a few weeks earlier, playing the organ at Mr. Dabrowski's funeral Mass. Her skin had looked healthy and her eyes had looked clear. And she had been just as infectiously good as she'd always been. I wish I had known.

Having dropped the church truck at the back of the church, I helped Pop-Pop set up the flowers. We had arrived about thirty minutes before the pallbearers, who would help us carry the casket up the steep stone steps of Our Lady and into the sanctuary. I brought in the Reserved signs, the register book, and prayer cards, and then both Pop-Pop and I walked through the sacristy, which connected the church and the rectory.

Father was standing on the rectory's porch, finishing off a cigarette. He flicked it into the bushes as soon as he saw us. "Don't want to make your expensive suits stink," he said, with an ornery grin.

I could tell he was slightly subdued. He would have normally followed that line with a deep laugh.

"You guys ready for a long day?"

"We're set up as much as we can be," Pop-Pop said. "The pallbearers will be here in fifteen, and we'll bring Joan in."

"She look good?" Father asked.

I told Father that Pop-Pop had made her look wonderful. Not only had Pop-Pop met with Joan's family, but he had also embalmed, dressed, and cosmetized Joan. He had invested hours into making her look the best he possibly could, and his work paid off.

"Well, I've had one of the most spiritual weeks I've ever experienced," Father started. "I had a dream the night after Joan died. It was one of those vivid dreams that feels like it's really happening. I saw her entering heaven and being greeted by Mary. Angels were singing as Mary led Joan to Jesus. What happened next is something I didn't expect. Jesus sat up, walked to Joan, and greeted her—just like you and I are doing right now."

He paused, and we waited. "After they talked for a little, Joan presented Jesus with a Christmas gift. The next part I can't explain, but I just knew that her gift was today. It was this funeral. Joan's gift to Jesus was everyone who comes today."

Like many funeral directors, my grandfather and father and I have listened to innumerable stories from families who tell us their dreams and visions and signs from their deceased loved ones. Through Pop-Pop's nearly seventy-year career, he had likely heard a thousand such stories.

And he believed nearly all of them.

I, on the other hand, don't. Or didn't.

—

My grandparents were in high school during World War II, and the default of their generation of white young people was a belief that held little space for doubts. The Nazis were bad and America was good. They didn't easily give in to doubt. Some of these believers were fundamentalists in the truest sense: believers who had a set of certainties that always went unquestioned.

They were fundamentalist believers in their system of morals and values, which were good and not merely for their own culture, but—they thought with equal parts pride and optimism—every other culture of the world. They were fundamentalist believers in their faith, which they believed represented the pinnacle of peace and goodness and God's love. They were fundamentalist believers in their leaders— community, religious, family, government—leaders who were never as evil as Adolf Hitler, Benito Mussolini, or Hideki Tōjō.

In that crowd of God-and-country believers, only a rare few gave space to doubt. They entertained the doubt, thought about it, and let it shape them. Yesterday's doubters are today's saints. Susan B. Anthony. Charles Darwin. Mahatma Gandhi. Albert Einstein. Sylvia Rivera. Rosa Parks. Martin Luther King Jr. People who questioned the status quo. My generation honors them through our own skepticism.

Today's world is very different from the world of the 1940s. Good and bad are no longer absolutes. Despite demagogues' attempts to paint their opposition as the enemy, the line between the heroes and the villains is nowhere as clear as it was when Hitler and Stalin were systematically exterminating entire people groups. In today's world, God is no longer a wise-looking white man sitting on a European-style throne. Even the word *family* is polysemous. The complexity of the world and lack of absolutes has only been reaffirmed by the lesson of the internet: humans are a diverse bunch with diverse cultures, diverse beliefs, and diverse morals. And very few of these very different people are as bad as we've thought.

So unlike Father Mick and my grandfather, I didn't naturally believe Father Mick's dream was a message sent directly from Jesus and Joan to us. When I hear the stories that families tell me of dreams and visions, I doubt. I am, however, very much like Pop-Pop in one aspect. He was a fundamentalist of belief, and I have become a fundamentalist of doubt. I believed Father Mick, in one sense. I *believed* he had indeed had the dream. But I also thought his dream was probably a product of wishful thinking. Father loved Joan—we all did—and that love for her and her life produced a vision where he saw everything he'd hoped for Joan: an eternity in heaven with Jesus.

Such visions, I would have said, are a coping method for the terrible reality that is death. Death is so sudden, and so final, that in order for humans to cope with mortality, they make up a place that is immortal and eternal: the afterlife.

Here's a two-question test for you:

What if the afterlife doesn't exist?

What if you don't live eternally?

Okay. Test over.

How did those questions make you feel? I'd guess that they make most of us feel uneasy, especially those who believe in an afterlife. Research suggests that the number of people who believe in the afterlife has remained relatively stable over the past couple of decades. Yet voices that unapologetically refute the existence of the afterlife have grown in number.

Seventeenth-century French moralist François de la Rochefoucauld wrote, "Death, like the sun, cannot be looked at steadily." As a skeptic, I've tried to look at death: to understand it, feel it. Looking with clear eyes at death is part of what I did in my first book, *Confessions of a Funeral Director*, and it remains my task in this one. But in this book I want to ask questions about the hereafter, and to tell the stories families have told me about all the ways their dead still speak.

This book isn't the same as some of the books on the afterlife that you could have picked up. Readers devour books like *Heaven Is Real* and *Ninety Minutes in Heaven* not because those books provide ample and reproducible evidence for the existence of life after death but because they confirm people's deepest wish to be free from mortality. To skeptics like me, all those books prove is that, to avoid nihilism, most people have to wear a death equivalent of sunglasses they call "heaven."

To reinforce belief in heaven and the afterlife, many people look for any pebble of confirmation. Over the course of a couple of decades, experimental psychologists Sheldon Solomon, Jeff Greenberg, and Tom Pyszczynski developed what they call "terror management theory." Based in the theoretical work of Ernest Becker, terror management theory starts with a few of Becker's propositions:

1. Like all biological life on earth, humans are wired to seek life and avoid death.

2. Unlike other biological life, humanity's somewhat unique creative and mental capacity makes us aware that we will die.

3. Our awareness of our own mortality can be softened through cultural worldviews, such as

the afterlife, that create both symbolic immortality and self-esteem.

4. Belief and adherence to that cultural worldview is how we manage our death anxiety.

Terror management theory posits that when other people call into question our cultural worldviews, we move into "worldview defense." This defense produces "vigorous agreement with and affection for those who uphold or share our beliefs (or who are similar to us) and equally vigorous hostility and disdain for those who challenge or do not share our beliefs (i.e., are different from us)."

I used to believe that terror management theory offered the only viable way to explain heaven—that is, that the afterlife was just a coping mechanism for humanity's fear of death. And for good reason. I've heard hundreds of funeral services in which preachers harness the fear of death to get the funeral attendants to "accept Christ." I've heard it so many times I could probably preach their message for them.

And on the day of Joan's funeral, as I listened to Father Mick finish telling us his dream of Joan and Jesus, I wondered if this dream was nothing more than a way for him to cope with the sudden death of someone he loved. My grandfather didn't share my doubt, however, because as soon as Father Mick was finished telling of his vision, Pop-Pop confidently told him, "God was showing you what was happening to Joan."

But the stories I have heard during my work as a funeral director, some of which I'll share with you in this book, complicate my doubt. They challenge my skepticism. The families I've met with make me ask questions: What if our dead remain with us in some way that my Western worldview had not prepared me to see? What if the hereafter isn't "up there"? What if the hereafter intersects with the here and now?

Perhaps all the claims that visions and dreams and connections to ancestors are "in your head"—perhaps those claims *themselves* are a massive oversimplification of what is actually happening. I'm a skeptic, not a misanthrope.

Some stories are even more believable than others because they happened to people who weren't looking for them. These kinds of stories don't just happen to religious people. And they rarely happen to people oppressed by the fear of death and grabbing for the afterlife to give them some peace. These experiences happen to people from every walk of life: to those who believe in the afterlife and to those who don't.

As it turns out, belief is not a prerequisite for having an experience with the afterlife. After listening to so many stories, I began to wonder if they might hold some kind of truth.

CHAPTER 2

AN UNSOLICITED VISION

It was Christmas Day in Southeast Pennsylvania, and it was snowing. Not the pretty kind of snow that gently blankets the countryside but the angry snow that wants to pound the earth into submission. This wasn't the white Christmas of Bing Crosby's dreams; it was the kind that could knock down trees, snap electrical lines, and offer the weather equivalent of Christmas coal. So my mom and dad decided it was in everyone's best interest if we exchanged gifts early in the day, before the storm could crank up its anger and cover the roads.

Christmas for my mom is an extension of her heart and soul. From August to December, she gathers gifts and plans festivities like it's a part-time job, pouring her money and thoughtfulness into each and every gift for me, my siblings, our spouses, and our kids. A love of the Christmas holiday ran in Mom's family, the Browns. Every year Pop-Pop and Mamaw Brown put up a Christmas tree with blue string lights wrapped around it. The blue lights gave it such a unique look that even just imagining it now brings a flood of childhood memories of me and my cousins opening presents in the room right next to the funeral home's chapel. Each year, it seemed like they put the tree up earlier than anyone else. I don't know if it was my Pop-Pop or Mamaw who got that tree up early, but my mom still embraces the tradition.

We arrived at my parents' house at seven in the morning. We opened gifts and ate cinnamon rolls. Opened some more gifts and ate more food. Around ten, the snow hit another gear, and so we all started to pack up our cars with our loads of new stuff and the leftover food Mom was sending home with us. I usually have to play Tetris in the trunk of my car. After about ten minutes of fighting the laws of physics, I finally stuffed the last gift into the trunk when I heard my dad yelp. It's the noise he has always used when he wants his kids' attention in an open-air setting. I pulled my head out of the trunk and saw Dad waving me back to the house. He had a certain look on his face—you know, the look you'd make if you were a funeral director and you just got a death call on Christmas Day during the beginning of a blizzard.

"I just talked to the hospice nurse. It's up past Morgan-town. The wife wants us to come because she's afraid if we don't come now, we won't be able to get there for a couple of days."

We always cross our fingers on holidays, hoping that we'll be able to spend them with our families. Sometimes it works out. Other times, we have to switch from the relaxed joy of a holiday to the suit and tie of the funeral director profession. I think, if most funeral directors are honest, we'll say it's not the tragic deaths that would cause us to quit this profession. It's that death teaches us over and over again how important life is, even while the death profession so often takes us *away* from those lives. Funeral directors who learn death's lesson often quit the business. They understand that life is too valuable to have it taken away by the awkward rhythms of death.

I dropped my wife, Nicki, and our son, Jeremiah, off at home, put on an old suit, and slipped on my snow boots just in case the car got stuck in the snow and I had to push. Our removal van wasn't cut out for this kind of snow. There was only one vehicle that had a chance: my grandfather's Chevy Suburban. So I called up Pop-Pop Wilde and made sure he was okay with us taking his Suburban out in a blizzard. Asking him to borrow the Suburban was more a formality than a necessity. He was always willing to lend out his stuff for the good of the funeral home.

I drove over to the garage that housed his Suburban, popped out the back seat, folded down the second row, and drove it across the street to the funeral home. Pop-Pop had been born in the funeral home and had lived there for most of his adult life. When he decided that it was time to move out of the funeral home, he bought the house across the street. His house had an open-air front porch that he had enclosed with windows, and he'd installed a small propane-fueled wall heater. That way he could sit out on his porch at any time of the year and look across the street to watch—often with a critical eye—what we were doing at the funeral home. Like his father before him, even when his body could no longer perform tasks at the funeral home, his eye was firmly fixed on us to make sure we did it right. Even on Christmas morning, I could see him through the snow, watching.

I backed the Suburban up to the prep room ramp, and Dad loaded our stretcher in the back. He threw a couple of shovels in the back in case we got stuck in a snow drift and climbed in the driver's seat.

—

The drive from Parkesburg to Morgantown usually takes about thirty minutes, but this trip took us close to an hour and a half. We crawled through the blinding snow that was beginning to drift deep over the wind-whipped Route 10. When we exited Route 10 and merged onto a back road, Dad hit a patch of ice and spun the Suburban 180 degrees into an embankment. If we had been going fast, it would have busted up the SUV. But we were going slow enough it only damaged our confidence in the prowess of our four-wheel drive Suburban. Dad had had enough of driving at that point, so we switched places and I drove the last couple of miles to the deceased's home.

Enosh "Noshi" Limen—that was his name. An odd name for Chester County, Pennsylvania, but one that has now gone down in the annals of Wilde Funeral Home's 170-year history as the man who died on Christmas Day in the middle of a blizzard. We pulled up to the ranch-style house, backed in as close to the front door as we could, and climbed out of the Suburban. I knocked on the front door loud enough to be heard over the blowing wind and snow and then peeked in the window. When I didn't see anyone coming, I made a quick check at the house number to make sure we were at the right place. (A recurring fear of mine is showing up at the wrong house and having to explain away the awkwardness of "Oops, I thought this was where the dead guy was.")

After thirty seconds or so of waiting, we knocked harder and louder, and this time our noise was answered.

"You guys look almost as miserable as I am," said the woman who opened the door. "I'm Gerda, Noshi's wife," she added, as we walked in and pulled the door shut behind us.

"I apologize in advance for the snow we're going to track into your house," I said as I looked at the small piles our boots left on the carpet.

"Snow's better than mud and much better than dog shit," Gerda said with an ornery smile.

She led us back to the bedroom where Noshi lay. As we walked down the hall, I noticed two things: there were no Christmas decorations, and there were tons of books. Smart books. I saw some older luminaries—William James, Charles Darwin, Sigmund Freud, Friedrich Nietzsche's books (in their original German)—and books on art, history, war, economics, and theater. This was the collection of a polymath.

One of the best ways to make a quick assessment of a person's likes and interests is to check out the books in their house. If books are in plain sight, the resident is offering you a peek into their minds. And I was excited by what I saw in Gerda and Noshi's house—really excited. Because if I could do anything in life—absolutely anything—I'd read nonstop, only breaking to hang out with friends and family, exercise, and eat meals with balanced macros. I'm one of those Casanova book buyers who has a ton of books but only reads the chapters that pique my interest. As soon as the excitement is gone, I'm on to the next book that interests me. The books in Gerda and Noshi's house—and there were hundreds of them—were not the books of a romantic book buyer. They had the well-worn look only created by a committed reader.

As we entered the room where Noshi lay, a well-dressed woman got up from her chair and greeted us with a pleasant smile and a handshake. "I'm Celeste, the hospice chaplain," she said. "I was at the home of Mr. Morris a few months back, and I remember you guys being so kind to the Morris family. I was glad when Gerda said that she was using your funeral home."

As I'd later learn, Celeste had a presence that could fill a room, but at this hour her presence was focused on Gerda and Noshi. She sat back down in her chair and took an unassuming posture. I remembered seeing Celeste at the Morris home, as well as at a few funerals at Mt. Zion AME Church in Atglen, her family's home church. We'd shared pleasantries in the past at funerals but nothing substantial enough for us to know each other's first names.

"Celeste is my angel," Gerda announced. "She's been here for the past twelve hours, keeping watch. She's here so that I wouldn't be alone with Noshi during the blizzard. I don't believe in angels, but Celeste has me reconsidering," she said, her head slightly tilted and eyes fixed on Celeste in appreciation.

Deathcare is a bit like marriage or parenthood: you might think of yourself as a good person when you begin, but it manages to lay bare all your deficiencies. It can bring out the absolute worst in us. Yet sometimes I meet people—whether hospice nurses, pastors, or friends of the family—who have been through the trials of deathcare and somehow come out better on the other side. If there are angels, I don't think we'll find them in heaven or on the clouds. They'll likely be near the beds of the dying and the dead, like Celeste.

"This is Noshi," Gerda said, as she turned her attention to the body of her recently deceased husband. Noshi lay on the bed with his mouth and eyes open. "We couldn't get them shut," Gerda said, reading our thoughts. Noshi had that sticky, humid, cancer smell. His face looked tired. It looked like the kind of dead body Hollywood can only try to copy. He was gaunt, and the pallor of his skin had hints of yellow. His eyes had lost their convexity and their shimmer. You could just make out his brown iris underneath the clouded cornea.

"He makes a good dead body." Gerda smiled, eliciting a snicker and headshake from Celeste. "Neither of my parents looked dead when they died. But Noshi did it right."

"Maybe the cancer changed the way he looked," my dad interjected. "But I don't recognize him or know anyone with the name. I don't think I've met you or Noshi before now. Have we met?"

Dad spoke with a shyness that he hoped would cover his embarrassment if they had and he didn't remember. Our funeral home only advertises if we're asked to "buy a spot" in the Little League calendar or the local youth center's fundraiser. All our business comes either through relationships or word of mouth. So if we don't know the person who died, it's likely that we know the person who recommended us.

"Noshi knew old Jim through the Parkesburg VFW," Gerda said. "Jim's either your dad or uncle?"

"He's my uncle. And I haven't introduced myself yet—the whole gale force winds and drifting snow has thrown me off," Dad continued. "I'm Bill, and this is my son, Caleb." Dad followed this with one of his favorite lines: "I used to be Wild Bill, but now I'm just Bill Wilde."

We all smiled. "And what are you, Caleb?" asked Gerda, setting me up for my one-liner.

"Oh, I'm the youngest of the bunch—you know, the least Wilde."

I must have used that line a hundred times by now. It takes most people a couple of seconds to realize the play on words, but despite Gerda's grief brain, she got it right away and laughed.

I'm pretty sure my dad hadn't noticed the lack of Christmas decorations or the vast array of books. But he did pick up on a framed document that hung in the hallway. Dad's a historian. I'd say amateur historian, because he doesn't have a degree and he doesn't study history for a living, except he could have if he had wanted to. His brain is wired to store any piece of historical information it hears, especially history that relates to the American Civil War, World War II, and Kentucky long rifles. When Gerda mentioned Noshi's involvement with the VFW, he jumped on that talking point.

"I saw Noshi's army discharge in the hall. Let me guess: Korean War?"

"Yup. He was stationed at Campbell Barracks in Heidelberg, Germany," Gerda announced. "That's where we met."

"Were you in a MASH unit, or WAC?"

"Neither. I was a student at Heidelberg University. I'm German."

Both Dad and I were taken back. Gerda had no discernible German accent. If anything, she had a slight Southern drawl. I could tell Dad had a thousand questions running through his head, but he kept them all in, saving them for a different time and place.

When we go on a house call for a removal, our conversations with the surviving loved ones often give us a CliffsNotes version of the deceased's life. We talk about a wide range of topics, with little depth in a short amount of time. On a normal removal, we might talk about the deceased's sickness, how long they lived at their residence, their marriage, hobbies, occupation, and anything else that seems natural. It puts the family at ease when we know a bit about their loved one's life. If we become proxy family, it's easier for them to trust us when we take the body of their father, mother, son, or daughter into our care.

Dad continued to the endgame of his army discharge observation. "If you have his DD214, bring it with you when we make arrangements and I'll get as many government benefits as I can for you."

"Can I ask you guys a question?" Gerda said suddenly.

Dad, preparing for a professional question, straightened up his posture and folded his hands together in the typical undertaker pose. "Go ahead," he said.

We waited a bit while Gerda collected herself. Then came the question that surprised us both.

"Do you guys believe in ghosts?" Gerda asked.

—

Questions like this are sensitive, vulnerable questions. It's almost akin to asking if someone believes in God. Some people believe very strongly in a yes, and others answer no just as strongly. Questions about ghosts and God become groupish questions ("groupish" is like selfish, but in group form). If your answer doesn't match the asker's belief, you're not a part of their community.

People in the yes group usually have an experience or a story to back their position, while those in the no group view ghosts—or God—as hallucinations at best, and exaggerations or lies at worst. One group tends to perceive the world through sense and intuition, and so they feel things in the world that the eye might not see. The other group tends to believe there's a natural explanation for most ostensibly supernatural phenomena.

After Gerda's question, Celeste tilted her head up to listen. She leaned forward in the chair and looked at my dad and me, like she had known this question was coming and was anticipating our reaction.

"I do," my dad chimed in. "I saw one when I was a teenager."

To this day, Dad claims he saw a ghost when he was on a Boy Scout campout deep in the hills of the Appalachians. On the first day of their weekend campout, some of the scouts went on a hike that snaked past an old burned-out tavern from a bygone era. There wasn't any talk of the tavern being haunted, nor were the boys hyped from campfire ghost stories. As they were looking at the tavern, all the boys saw a strange light and a female figure emerge from the ruins.

Dad is an honest person, and I've never doubted what he thought he saw. I've actually asked some of Dad's scouting friends who saw the ghost if their *adult* selves still believe what their *kid* selves saw. All of them concur with my dad: they maintain that they saw something that would best be described as a ghost.

When it comes to ghosts and spirits, I'm a skeptic. I believe our brains have blind spots, especially when they're loaded with the clouding of death. It's a bit like when a hearse is loaded with a casket: you can't see out the back window, and you can't always see out the side windows on the rear doors. Anytime you're driving a hearse and merging onto a congested highway, it feels like an act of trust. You can look in both rearview mirrors, honestly and intelligently believe that there's no car on your right or left—and then *honk!*—the car in your blind spot reminds you of their existence.

There are exploitable misfires in our brains that cause us to *not* see some things, and—at times—to see things that don't actually exist. If you've experienced death, you know what I mean. We can be the most honest and intelligent people, and the deaths of loved ones still have a way of bending reality.

Grief is a strong feeling. Strong feelings can be bad things to a critical mind because they cloud judgment. For instance, sometimes when our minds are loaded down with death or fear or desperation, our brains honestly think they see things that do not exist. These illusions are similar to desert mirages. Like the nomad in the hot desert who has seen one too many mirages, some of us start to lose trust in our own brains and the way they can misinterpret reality. So with regard to stories of ghosts and spirits, I'm like the nomad. I've heard one too many tall tales to trust people's perceptions.

Gerda seemed surprised by my dad's answer to her question about ghosts, but she went on. "Well, I *don't* believe in ghosts, so this experience is causing no small amount of cognitive dissonance," she said in an academic tone.

If we had caught her last week, I imagine she might have been asking this as a groupish question—expecting her listeners to agree with her on the ridiculousness of a belief in ghosts. But today, it wasn't.

"I was sitting in this chair by the bed, watching the snow blow past the window," she said. "Celeste was in the other room, sleeping on that old sofa. My eyes scanned the room and there, at the foot of the bed, stood Noshi's parents. His dad stood here on this side, and his mother stood on the other."

Gerda spoke matter-of-factly. She seemed removed from her own experience, like she was just reporting what she saw and not trying to convince us one way or another. It was like she was offering an anthropologist's field report. "I talked to them, but there was no response, only a general feeling of warmth and goodness," she said. "I was about to get up out of my chair to see if I could touch them, when I suddenly realized I no longer heard Noshi's labored breathing. I looked down at him, and some intuitive sense told me that he was gone. I felt his chest, looked for any signs of breathing, and by the time I was done searching for vitals, his parents were gone—along with him."

I glanced over at Dad to scan his facial expression and see if he was as intrigued as I was. He had his head tilted to the side, which I thought was odd until I noticed that when I looked back at Gerda, my head was tilting too. I remembered reading somewhere that a tilted head is a nonverbal signal for deep interest. Gerda noticed too and kept talking.

"Even after seeing Noshi's parents standing over his bed before he died, I figure it's likely they were a product of my lack of sleep and my overimaginative brain," Gerda said, adding, "although, to be clear, it's not because I've been drinking ayahuasca."

I looked at my dad to see if ayahuasca registered in his brain; he had the same I'm-not-sure-what-that-is-but-I-understand-what-you're-saying look that I had. To save you an internet search, ayahuasca is a strong hallucinogenic drug that contains the chemical DMT (N,N-Dimethyltrypt-amine), which many believe is created by the body when the body nears death and is thought to be a possible cause of near-death experiences.

"So as soon as he died, I called for Celeste and she came into the room," Gerda continued. "Celeste's a spiritual person." She turned her head to Celeste and said, "I'm pretty sure you're okay with me telling them you're spiritual."

Celeste nodded in approval and said with a chuckle, "It does help explain why I'm a chaplain."

Gerda turned back to us. "And she still manages to tolerate me: a well-informed, assertive atheist," she said. "But I won't deny that she somehow knew. Seeing the look on my face, she said, 'Something mysterious and wonderful just happened.' I told her Noshi died, that I saw his parents, and that my mind likely concocted the whole thing."

Celeste stood up. "I told her—and I'll remind her now—" she said, her voice projecting louder than it had before, "your first job isn't to interpret your experience. Your first job is to listen to it."

Celeste's voice was a confluence of something fresh and something deep and ancient, of pain and joy, of authority and love. I got the feeling that she could tell you anything— that she didn't like your shirt or that she disagreed with your politics—and that, no matter what she said, you would feel safe.

This wasn't the first time I had met Celeste, but this was the first time I got a little introduction to her personality. Her family had generational ties to Bethany AME Church back on Green Street in Parkesburg and Mt. Zion AME Church in Atglen, where we had directed a few funeral services for members of her extended family.

Having stayed with Gerda for the past twenty-four hours or more, Celeste had earned a bit of say-so in Gerda's life. "And just because you don't believe in God doesn't mean that you can't connect to your ancestors," she continued. "They are two different things, you know—although some of your ancestors were Nazis, so maybe it'd be best if you left them alone," Celeste added with a laugh.

Gerda walked over to Celeste, wrapped her arm around Celeste's waist, and said, "I love you, too, honey. And just because I don't believe it doesn't mean it's not real. It just means I haven't found a good explanation." They shared one of those laughs we in the funeral business know so well: laughs that happen around death when the subject isn't funny but simply because your body needs to feel something good. It becomes an automatic survival function. You breathe, your heart beats, and when someone dies—for some odd evolutionary reason—you cry and you laugh.

After a few more moments, Gerda let us know she was ready for us to make the removal. Dad and I went out into the blizzard to get our stretcher and brought it into the house, tracking fresh snow across the rug. We wheeled it to Noshi. As is my custom, I invited Gerda to help us if she wished to take part. Dad grabbed Noshi's waist, I grabbed his feet, Gerda cradled his head, and Celeste pushed him toward us as we slid him from his bed and onto the stretcher. Gerda kissed his face for the last time, and we covered his body with the cot cover.

Dad gave Gerda a hug and explained that we'd need her to come into the funeral home, sign some authorization forms, and give us the information we need for the death certificate.

"We should probably wait a few days for the streets to clear. How about we call you in a couple of days to set up a time?" Dad suggested.

As we exited the house, I thought about saying Merry Christmas, but it didn't seem appropriate. So we said a simple goodbye and trekked out into the blowing snow with Noshi.

We let the SUV warm up and then we slowly started our journey home. Dad and I were silent for the first ten minutes of our ride as our eyes and minds took in the blinding conditions and drifting snowbanks. When we finally started to get a feel for the road, Dad asked, "What do you think about Gerda seeing Noshi's parents?"

"I'm not sure," I answered. "But I do know I really liked Gerda and Celeste. I feel like I could learn a lot from each of them."

We made it back to Parkesburg nearly two hours after we left Gerda's house. As we rolled Noshi into the prep room and tucked the Suburban back into Pop-Pop's garage, we knew Pop-Pop was likely peering at us through his porch. We made it to our homes in time to watch Mother Nature's Christmas gift turn into a foot of snow.

CHAPTER 3

KEPT ALIVE BY A FUNERAL

I told my dad and Pop-Pop that I wanted to make funeral arrangements with Gerda because I was interested in her story about seeing Noshi's parents and I liked her vibe. I had been making funeral arrangements sporadically with families throughout the first ten years of working at the funeral home. In my twenties and early thirties, it never made sense for me to meet with families since my dad and grandfather likely already knew them. Dad and Pop-Pop had gone to school with many in the community. Pop-Pop attended Parkesburg's own school from first through twelfth grade, while Dad went to the Parkesburg school from first to eighth and then attended high school at the newly consolidated Octorara High School. That's where my dad met my mom. Pop-Pop and Dad had both volunteered with the Parkesburg fire department. Pop-Pop was involved in the Masonic lodge and the Lions Club, while Dad was active in a number of nonprofits and charities.

I only went to our local school district until the fourth grade. In fifth grade, I was sent to a private school, and I eventually graduated from a private high school half an hour's drive from home. Going to a school outside our area put me at a relational disadvantage in knowing the Parkesburg community. Instead of having preexisting relationships, I had to learn names and connections on the fly while working funerals. I suppose I could have joined the lodge or the Lions Club or the fire company, but my introverted personality won out.

Pop-Pop's health had started to slowly fail in his early eighties, opening the door for me to start meeting with families on my own more consistently. For ten years, I had watched Pop-Pop walk families through the difficult conversations that happen during funeral arrangements. I had studied him. I had watched how he moved the conversation along, how he expertly used a gentle touch on the arm or back to comfort the grieving people he was meeting with. Pop-Pop's deep listening skills were spot on. But what made families comfortable with him was that he always knew when to fill the space with his own stories. It might seem self-centered to be telling stories about yourself while meeting with a grieving family, but sometimes filling empty space, even if you're filling it with your own stories, is its own act of grace.

"Go ahead and meet with Gerda," Pop-Pop said encouragingly. "I remember Noshi from the American Legion. He always had some whiskey by his side at the Legion. Nice guy with a weird name."

So after waiting about three days for Gerda's road to be cleared by snowplows, salt, and sun, I set up a time to meet with her and finalize the arrangements. As happened during most holiday seasons, the dead were piling up at the funeral home. This postholiday increase in deaths is expected in the funeral industry, although there really isn't one explanation as to why it happens.

Gerda arrived at our funeral home on time, which was an impressive feat considering the road conditions were still making travel difficult. I greeted her at the door with a smile.

"My Siberian huskies are still on Christmas holiday, so I had to drive myself," she said, chuckling, with that humor that I adored the first time I met her.

"Do they get a paid holiday?" I played along.

"After 'the man' drove them like dogs for years, they finally unionized," she said. "Now they have more holidays than workdays. I give them free food, a place to rest, and I even clean up their shit."

"Is there an opening on their team? Because my job makes me work during blizzards," I said with a smile, hoping she'd know I wasn't complaining.

"And on Christmas too!" she shot back. "You do have a tough job. I'll ask the dogs when I get home."

After I hung up her coat on the coatrack, we sat down and continued the chitchat. Her childlike nature made her playful, but it also made her transparent. With Gerda, the conversations were either playful banter or stark honesty.

"I noticed two things when I entered your home," I said to Gerda. "I noticed that there were no Christmas decorations. And I was amazed by your eclectic library."

"Well, the no-Christmas part is because Noshi and I are atheists," she replied. "Or should it be, 'I'm an atheist and Noshi *was* an atheist'? My grammar has yet to catch up with Noshi's death. And we don't have children or grandchildren. We never had a reason to make Christmas a part of our lives. The eclectic library part is because Noshi and I tried to learn something new every day. Learning and reading made us both happy."

"Back at your home, you mentioned that you met Noshi while you were going to Heidelberg University," I said. "What did you study?"

"I was finishing my graduate degree in anthropology. Anthropology was a pretty broad field in the early 1950s. Not as specific as it is today. It was the track you took if you were simply interested in people. For you to notice our library, I'm assuming you like books?" she said with keen interest.

"I just finished seminary—a Christian seminary—and I'm starting a postgrad degree called Death, Religion, and Culture," I said. "If I had a choice to be anything I wanted, I'd be a full-time student. A dream that I will fulfill if I ever retire."

"You've studied a God that I don't believe exists," Gerda said matter-of-factly. "And I study people, many of whom believe in God. I suspect we can still be friends?" She smiled.

"We can," I said. "For sure. And it's nice to know that if we do become friends, I don't have to buy you a Christmas present."

"Untrue. If you're a good Christian, you'll get me a wonderful gift even if I don't deserve it." Then she flashed some theological verbiage: "If you're a great Christian, you'll give me your life, like Jesus. But—" She stopped midsentence and grinned. "I'll gladly settle for the gift of a free cremation."

"You know that in America, capitalism always trumps our Christianity, right?" I replied. "So, I'm going to say no to the free cremation." That line made us both smile because of its stark—and sad—truth.

"Well, let's get on with it," she said.

—

Before I start making funeral arrangements with families, I always like to tell them a bit about the process ahead: what we're going to do, what they should expect. It's a learned kindness to give bereaved people a sense of order. Their lives have been full of chaos over the last couple of days, and clarity can be comforting.

After I laid out the decisions and schedule ahead of us, Gerda let me know she was already skeptical of my work. She had read Jessica Mitford's classic exposé of the funeral industry, *The American Way of Death*, she told me. And that's all she needed to say.

Mentioning Jessica Mitford at most funeral homes is like talking about Voldemort at Hogwarts. Mitford struck an honest and needed blow to the funeral industry. In her 1963 investigation of undertakers, who she portrays as entirely motivated by profit, she didn't just do the usual, "There's some really bad people in the funeral industry, but most of them are good." No. She thought the whole thing was inherently exploitive, and that even good-hearted men and women lose their goodness when they join the industry.

"I've read most of it," I replied, "and I own a copy of the Federal Trade Commission investigative reports that it prompted." Mitford's muckraking investigation resulted in the consumer-protective Funeral Rule, which requires that funeral homes are transparent about pricing.

"I agree with most of what I've read in the book," I told Gerda. I wanted to assure her that I have scruples about the industry too. Like her, I'm disgusted by the upselling, the price gouging, and the profiteering by many funeral directors. "And I'll happily give you a free cremation because we're friends," I said, with all honesty. (I'd later remove the "professional service fee" as well. I've got a business to run, but I do my best to maintain a safe distance from being perceived as a capitalist.)

Offering people free funeral-related stuff doesn't always go over as smoothly as you might think. Some grieving people actually feel a need to spend money when a loved one dies. Maybe they want to feel like they financially took care of their dead. Maybe they don't want to feel like they owe us something. Maybe they don't want to be perceived as needy. Maybe they equate spending money with spending love. Maybe they just want the comfort of capitalism.

Gerda was no different. "Fine," she said. "I'll take the free cremation, but you'll be accepting a donation in return."

She continued. "Also, I don't want a funeral for Noshi." And in true Mitfordian flair, she followed with, "I just want the cheapest cremation you got, and I'll donate whatever all your other customers give when they get the same."

As Gerda and I talked, it became apparent that her desire for "the cheapest cremation you got" wasn't just founded on principle but also on practicality. Noshi and Gerda had been living off their monthly Social Security payments. His retirement had been slowly eaten away by the rising cost of living. And the monthly expenditures of their car, food, and other bills left little for funeral expenses. It's an all-too-common story for those at Noshi and Gerda's age.

Our funeral home has always found a way to work with families in legitimate financial need. It's part of our reputation. That ability has been enabled by our staying power and frugality. We don't have a shiny new funeral home with a big mortgage, we don't get paid massive salaries, and we've never been about the bottom line. We've been around for nearly 170 years, and all our debts and mortgages have been paid off by older generations of Wildes, who often worked two jobs to make ends meet. You could say we are a blue-collar funeral home, and we've used our hard work and frugality to lower our prices and help those in real need.

I had Gerda sign the cremation authorization form and the FTC disclosure form prompted by Mitford's investigation. I gave her a hug, and she promised me she'd be back in a month with her donation.

—

A couple of weeks later, I was sitting in my office at the funeral home doing some paperwork when the doorbell rang. I put down my work and walked to the front door. There I found Gerda waiting on the other side, check in hand.

"You guys like money, right?"

I smiled and replied, "Do you know anyone who doesn't?"

We walked back to the office computer so I could chicken-peck the numbers into our dated funeral service software. While printing out her receipt, I asked Gerda how she was doing. In most settings outside a funeral home, such a question would generally be met with "Good," or "I'm fine, thanks"—even though we know that's not always the case. But here in a funeral home, such questions often receive refreshingly honest answers, especially when the bereaved, like Gerda, are already honest.

"I'm afraid," she said bluntly. "I'm a seventy-seven-year-old widow, and I'm afraid."

"Go on," I prompted.

"Over the past month, I've found it harder and harder to speak Noshi's name with my friends. I get the feeling that some people think I should be starting to get over my grief."

She looked at her hands. "I mean, I was married to him for over fifty years," she said, her face red. "And over fifty years of love and togetherness isn't shut off in a couple of weeks."

Her irritability changed a little, as she acknowledged that her friends' reluctance to talk about Noshi came from good intentions. "I think some don't talk about him because they think it will upset me. It might make me cry, but they're good tears. I don't think people understand that. Talking about him keeps him alive."

She straightened her back and let flow a stream of thoughts. Throughout my interactions with Gerda, her voice had always been controlled. Even when we had picked up Noshi, she had spoken evenly. Not once had I heard her voice shake from emotion. Until now.

"You know, I don't believe in heaven," she said. "I don't believe in a soul. Cartesian dualism is dead. You know that nobody has found the incorporeal part of a person, right? Because it's not there. I don't believe in an afterlife, where the souls of the dearly departed congregate and wait for their family and friends."

She kept talking, like she had planned out what she was going to say. "Caleb, speaking about Noshi is my way to an afterlife. People these days talk about their sex lives like it's nothing. They talk about their sicknesses, their feelings, their problems. We never did that when I was young, and it's a welcome change. Guys coming back from the war repressed their emotions, men were taught to hide their sicknesses, and talking about sex was taboo. We talk about those topics now. But *death?* We haven't changed. We still dance around it with platitudes and euphemisms. We're even more afraid—I think 'afraid' is the right word?—to talk about the *dead* than we are to talk about *death.* We can keep death at a distance. We can philosophize about it and read about it. But when we talk about a dead person, it's real. We don't do it. And it's dishonest. We think about them all the time in our private moments, but as soon as we make it public, the room goes silent."

Gerda took a breath and continued. "People wonder if something's wrong with you: maybe you're too depressed or maybe you're even losing it. I love the transparency today. But once we bury or cremate our dead, that's it. It's done. We shouldn't talk about them. Most people believe it's God's job to keep the dead alive in the afterlife. But as an atheist, I believe it's *my* job … and my friends are failing me. I want to talk about him, and I need my friends to help me."

I didn't have anything to say. And I certainly didn't want to stop Gerda from talking. This was an unguarded moment. It was something she needed. It was a privilege for me. It was human holy. Human sacred.

"So I'm just going to keep saying his name," Gerda told me. "I'm going to keep talking about Noshi. I'm going to keep him alive."

Gerda finished her thoughts, and her body sunk down in the chair. I assured her that speaking about Noshi was exactly what she should do.

"Have you thought about having a funeral?" I pried. "You don't need me, of course. I'm talking about at simple service at your house, with your closest friends."

"I don't want a funeral," she declared. "Noshi didn't want a funeral. He didn't want all the pomp and fanfare. He just wanted something simple, like a direct cremation," she said.

"But it could be simple," I pushed. "There doesn't have to be fanfare. You could share some stories about Noshi. You could ask some of your friends to share some stories. You could serve some of his favorite foods. Display some of his favorite books."

"I don't know," she followed. "Noshi always said, 'Just burn my ass.'"

She was silent for a moment. "But maybe I do need this."

—

If I'm honest, the funeral industry is to blame for the fact that "just burn my ass" is an increasingly popular sentiment. With all the expenses, hoopla, pomp, and stuffy professionalism that we've thrown into funerals—well, we funeral directors have outpaced and outclassed the majority of people, who would rather spend $10,000 on something that isn't going to be buried in the ground.

Shiny caskets, designer-suit-clad funeral directors, and funeral mansions that have begun to replace funeral homes: these no longer represent what wealth and prosperity and well-being look like to most people. "Wealth" used to look like Rolex watches, Prada handbags, and McMansions. But the conservation movement has begun to redefine wealth and value. These days, wealth is less directed toward things—especially things that aren't environmentally friendly, like a thousand-pound concrete vault in the ground into which an embalmed body is placed—and more toward education and opportunities and travel. Things that represent the new perception of wealth tend to be more sustainable, like a Prius or Tesla, or locally sourced food, or renewable energy sources. When it comes to death, the wealthy have begun to choose the more sustainable and less showy route of cremation.

Cremation fits the cultural ethos, and it is indeed greener than many other burial options. I understand that. But the "no funeral" idea that sometimes accompanies cremation—well, I think that approach grates against our humanity. I think something is lost when we don't gather to remember our dead.

Funerals are like midwives to an afterlife that is being born. They are a starting point for grief sharing, a starting point for making acceptable any talk about the dead. Funerals, at their core, are essential for "death positivity"—the perspective that encourages people to talk more openly about death. Funerals invite the memory of the dead—and sometimes the dead body itself—into the spaces of the living.

In fact, the more we skirt funerals, the more we move away from a death-positive posture. The more we bypass funerals, the more we isolate ourselves from the empathy of our community. The more we remove funerals from our community, the more we stunt the growth and weaken the connections of our individual, family, and community life.

Then again, these are thoughts from a funeral director, so take them with a grain of salt.

Gerda considered my words, likely weighing how much of my opinion was shaped by my profession and therefore how much they could be trusted. "Okay, Caleb," Gerda said, pushing herself out of her chair. "I will do it. And I do want you there—but not as a funeral director. As a friend."

"I'll most certainly come," I said. "I'll be honored. Let me know when you want to set the date."

CHAPTER 4

MORE THAN OURSELVES

"Caleb, we have a house call," my dad said over the phone. "Are you close to the funeral home?"

"I'm home," I said. "Who is it?"

"A guy by the name of Dwayne Kohler. Don't know him, but his wife and family are ready for us."

"Okay, I'll see you soon."

I pulled into the funeral home parking lot where Dad was waiting for me in the passenger's seat of the removal van. A half hour later we were rolling into Dwayne Kohler's parking lot, and I was backing through the maze of cars on and around their parking lot, inching as close to the front door as possible.

We were met by Dwayne's two daughters, who led us back to the master bedroom where Dwayne lay. He was a small guy in his midsixties, no more than 150 pounds. There was a rolled hand towel underneath his chin to keep his mouth closed, and the hospice nurse had dressed him in a fresh gown after she cleaned him up. I immediately noticed that Dwayne's hands and feet were wrapped in bandages, which usually means that the deceased has fragile skin that easily rips—unlikely, given Dwayne's relatively young age—or he or she had diabetic necrotic tissue.

Sheena, Dwayne's wife, was at his bedside running her fingers through his hair and whispering words that were just quiet enough that I couldn't make out what she was saying. He was lying in his own queen-sized bed, which was unusual, since nearly all home hospice patients are placed in fully adjustable medical beds provided by hospice. But the reason Dwayne wasn't in a medical bed quickly became apparent: Sheena had been sleeping on the other side of the queen, not leaving his side day or night during his final days.

After Dad and I stood silently at the bedside for thirty seconds or so, Sheena acknowledged us with her eyes. Without saying anything to us, she turned her eyes back to Dwayne and proceeded to give us a synopsis of their relationship.

"We got married right after he came back from Vietnam. He was a fucking mess," she said, with a slight grin, like she took some small pleasure dropping the f-bomb in front of complete strangers.

It didn't make me uncomfortable, though. These honest moments—these moments that happen between strangers at deathbeds and funerals—are the main reasons I've stayed in deathcare. It's like all the superficiality is washed away by the tide of death. All that remains is vulnerability and honesty, the bedrock of our humanity.

Death strips us emotionally naked. In fact, I have a recurring nightmare that I show up to work a funeral with no clothes on. There's so much context and decorum woven into funeral services, from the color of my dress shirt (only white), to the way I hold my hands (*never* in my pockets), to how I talk (low, steady, and calm), to the expressions on my face (I still remember being rebuked by a family member for smiling). Part of the "why" behind the outward decorum for both funeral service workers and those in attendance at funerals is compensation for the inward nakedness. That's my theory, anyway. Death is a kind of nakedness. And some of us feel ashamed of our nakedness, even embarrassed. Others, like Sheena, stand unashamed in their nakedness. It's a sign of their love, a sign of their humanity.

"The first ten years of our marriage were shit," she continued. "Undiagnosed PTSD. Well, PTSD wasn't a thing back then. After ten years of shit, he went to counseling. Bravest thing he ever did. To admit he needed help. We even did couples therapy up until a year ago, when he started to go downhill. It saved our marriage. We are so strong. And I love him more than anything."

She took her eyes off Dwayne and pointed them back at us. "Promise you'll take care of him."

"We'll treat him like he's our family," my dad replied. It's a line he has used a thousand times, but he still manages to imbue it with meaning.

His statement is true in a few ways. The gene pool of our area is pretty isolated. We're not Amish, but Parkesburg people like my family usually stay in the area, and many have family roots that go back many generations. And since most of us don't leave the area, and since not many people are lining up to move to the burgeoning metropolis that is not Parkesburg, we have to be careful who we marry—which is exactly where my dad went with his next line.

"We're probably related to you guys anyway," Dad concluded. Whether we are actually related doesn't actually matter, because the comfort and humor of the whole idea that we're one big family has its desired effect on most everyone who hears Dad's line—including Sheena, who nodded her head in approval.

Dwayne was going to be cremated. So when we got back to the funeral home, I felt his chest area for a pacemaker and found nothing. If he had a pacemaker, I would have had to remove it. Those buggers explode like a shotgun shell when they're cremated ... a lesson I've learned. Twice.

I unwrapped the bandages from his hands to check for rings. While forgetting to remove a pacemaker is a forgivable offense, forgetting to remove a ring before cremation is an act that has no mulligan. What I found surprised me: his fingers were necrotic. I had seen diabetic tissue necrosis, but a limb is usually amputated before it gets this bad.

I took the bandages off the right hand, mainly looking to make sure there weren't any rings on that hand, but I was also curious to see if that hand was necrotic as well. It was worse. Black skin. Shriveled. And only two fingers remained on a hand that bore little resemblance to human flesh. Maybe you've seen the photographs of bog bodies—bodies that have been naturally mummified in peat bogs? That type of shrivel. It looked like that.

Part of me wanted to unwrap his feet, just to see what damage had been done to his toes. But there was no pragmatic reason to see what was hidden underneath those dressings, so I let them be. Had he lived any longer, I'm sure his hands and feet would have been removed. He would have been wheelchair bound and mostly dependent upon others to do his daily tasks: eating, bathing, going to the bathroom, brushing his teeth, combing his hair.

I met with Sheena and their two daughters, Diane and Joy, the following morning to make funeral arrangements.

As is my custom, I asked questions about the deceased's final days. It allows me to get to know families a little more and understand where they are in the process, both practically and psychologically. It's the little details I'm interested in: Have you been able to sleep the last couple of days? Have you found time to eat? Was your loved one able to communicate with you until the end? Did this all happen quickly, or was it a slow, downhill process?

As we talked, Sheena and her daughters painted a picture of a man who was a fighter. This poor guy had it all. Belying his thin frame, he had developed type 2 diabetes in his mid-fifties. Diabetic kidney disease arrived in his early sixties, and soon the heart problems came along.

"I'm going to beat this," he would tell his daughters time and time again. "I'm going to beat this for your mother." He ate better, exercised more, was faithful with his meds. But his efforts simply prolonged the inevitable instead of curing it—an accomplishment nonetheless. As things progressively got worse, he dug in deeper because he vowed not to "quit." That was, after all, the mantra of his life's work. He had made it through Vietnam. He had worked through marital problems. He had gotten help for his PTSD. Dwayne didn't know "quit."

A year earlier, Dwayne's heart problems had become so severe that they could only be fixed with surgery. Even though the doctors gave him only a 30 percent chance of making it through the surgery, he decided to do it. He survived surgery, but it left him weaker than he was before. Soon the necrosis came. The doctors recommended that his hands and feet be amputated.

"That's when we had a heart-to-heart talk with him," Diane said. Diane was the more talkative of the two daughters. With her serious demeanor, Joy appeared to contradict the promise of her name. They both recounted to me what they had told him. As they narrated those conversations, I could tell that Joy was the realist. "Dad, you're a strong man," they told their father. "You never gave up. You've loved us until the end. And Dad, it's okay to die. Don't look at this as a battle lost; look at it as an honorable discharge."

"I want to keep going because I love your mom," he told them. Both the daughters' and the mother's eyes started to well up with tears as they recounted the conversation.

"We told him that she knows," Joy said. "We told him that knowing when enough is enough isn't the same as giving up."

He eventually made peace with the idea of death and stopped dialysis, they told me. Toward the end, Dwayne welcomed death.

Because death isn't a failure. Because it's okay to die. Because death does not turn you into a loser or a failed warrior.

—

We scheduled the memorial service for the coming Saturday, with an hour of visitation prior to the service. The day of the service arrived, and with it a hysterical phone call. My phone rang at 7:30 in the morning, and I answered it. It was Diane.

"Caleb ..." Diane could hardly get the words out. "She's dead."

"Who's dead?" I asked, drawing a total blank as to who "she" could be.

"Mom!" Diane said. "Mom's dead! Joy and I came over to help her get ready and take her to the funeral home. And the coffee wasn't on. And we didn't smell her perfume—the cheap stuff she sprays on after her shower. We walked back to her bedroom, and ... well, she's dead! The same place Dad died."

Diane's panic switched me into high gear funeral-director mode. It's a mode that all funeral directors have but only access on occasion. In those moments we act like outnumbered parents on a school field trip, who spout off orders with a confidence that outpaces the fact they have no idea how in the hell they'll ever keep all these kids alive.

"What do we do?" Diane was saying. "Can you guys come get her? And what do we do about Dad's funeral?"

I took a deep breath, stuttered a little over the phone, and suddenly my mind switched into gear. "Okay, so the first thing you need to do is call 911. We can only come to the house if your mom's doctor or the coroner signs off. As to the funeral: let's wait and see. Stay there with your mom until the coroner comes, and we'll take it from there. Today's going to be messy and confusing, but we'll all do the best we can."

"Okay," Diane said, with slightly less panic in her voice. She paused, and I prepared to end the call and get started on planning for a day of unknowns.

"And Caleb—there's one more thing," Diane stammered, her voice uneven. "I think she killed herself to be with Dad."

"Shit," I blurted out before I could think. My reaction surprised me. Before working in the funeral business, I had never cursed. I could step in dog crap and track it all over a Persian carpet, and I might utter a "darn" or a "dang." Now I had to watch my mouth exactly because of moments like this. It's as if being around all that death was stripping me of any pretense of polite speech. Maybe I'd soon be dreaming about showing up to work a funeral both naked and cursing.

"Sorry," I said. "I try to keep my words professional, so I apologize for my expletive. It's just ... well, I hadn't thought of that."

"My mom liked curse words, so it's totally appropriate."

"Yes. I do remember that," I said, with a grin. "Okay. Call 911 and we'll go from there."

An hour later, Diane called me back. "The coroner's going to take Mom. Mom's doctor wouldn't sign off. I told the coroner that Mom had regular checkups. No blood pressure problems, no heart issues, nothing. She was the exact opposite of Dad. I think the coroner might be leaning toward suicide as the cause of death too, especially after I told her how close Mom and Dad were and that today was his funeral. She didn't say 'suicide,' but it's the only thing that makes sense, right? They're going to do some toxicology tests and an autopsy, and those will tell us."

"Did you find any pill bottles emptied out?" I asked.

"I didn't see anything," she answered. "The coroner looked around too. It's weird because I don't know what she used if she did commit suicide. That part is weird, but we'll find out."

"I just want to let you know that toxicology reports usually take a couple of weeks, which is tough," I said. "I know you want to know right now. It's hard to wait, but—again, I'm just preparing you—we'll have to wait to get official results."

"Okay. I get it," Diane said. "It's just so strange," she mused. "I mean, it's almost poetic, like Romeo and Juliet."

"Is the coroner leaving?" I asked.

"They're finishing up."

I decided to broach the decision that loomed before us. "Do you want to continue on with your dad's service?" I asked, as gently as I could.

"We're dressed for it, and there's no way the word will get out that it's canceled," Diane said. "This might seem silly, but all those flowers ... they'll just die ... and the people who sent them ... well, I just want to do it. Joy agrees."

"We're ready for you," I said. "The lights are on, the heat's up—and our minibar is open."

Diane snickered a bit. We said goodbye and hung up.

Later that day Diane and Joy pulled into the funeral home parking lot right on time, just as planned—except for one thing, one very significant thing: they weren't chauffeuring their mom. That job belonged to the coroner, who was taking their mom to the county morgue for an autopsy and a toxicology test.

The visitation and funeral were so somber and so laborious for Diane and Joy, who were not only accepting condolences from family and friends but were continuously asked, "Where's your mom?" Eventually we just started telling people as soon as they entered the funeral home that Sheena had died that very morning. Nobody who attended knew what to say, but everyone gave hugs liberally.

By the end of the service, as the daughters were leaving the funeral home, they had the thousand-yard stare. I asked them if they could come over tomorrow to make arrangements for Sheena. They nodded yes.

We said goodbye, and as they left, I offered a line that momentarily snapped them out of the stare. "You guys have been at the funeral home so often lately that your mail's gonna start coming here."

—

One month after Sheena died, the final death certificate arrived through the funeral home's front door mail slot. Death certificates are now handled mostly online, but this death happened before this was common.

A death certificate is such an intimate document, especially when a death is sudden and no one knows what caused it. When that final death certificate arrives from the coroner's office, I always feel like opening it is almost morbid voyeurism. Except it's part of our job. Some of the causes and manners of death become deep secrets. I know a few people in our area who died from less-than-respectable circumstances. But sometimes the family didn't want anyone to know, so they told everyone their loved one died of a heart attack or a stroke—anything to keep the deceased's golden image undamaged.

But we funeral directors know. Your funeral director knows everything ... so be nice to us.

Anyway, my dad opened up the envelope and unfolded Sheena's death certificate. "Look at this," he said, handing it to me. "I've never seen this cause of death on a death certificate."

I walked over to Dad and peered down at the certificate to see what was so interesting. The check box for "natural death" was checked off. This was significant, because it meant Sheena's death wasn't suicide.

I moved my eyes over to the cause of death and saw what had intrigued my dad. The cause read "stress-induced cardiomyopathy."

Like my dad, I had never seen this cause on a death certificate. But unlike my dad, I knew exactly what it was.

I called Diane, since she was listed as the next of kin, and asked if the coroner had contacted her.

"Talked to her yesterday," Diane said.

"It wasn't a suicide, which explains why you didn't find anything around the house," I said.

"Joy and I had already settled on it being suicide, and we'd both made peace with it," Diane replied. "So that was a surprise."

"How did the coroner explain the cause of death to you?" I inquired.

"She told me that Mom didn't have any blocked arteries or valve problems, and she didn't have any history of high blood pressure or heart problems. But they did find a rupture in her ventricle wall, which was apparently caused by stress."

"You know stress-induced cardiomyopathy goes by another name, right?" I said. "Not to get heady, but I wrote my postgrad thesis on a related topic."

"I haven't really looked into it," Diane said. "But it makes sense that she died from stress—with Dad's death, and with how little sleep she had while sleeping in the same bed as him. I guess stress is more powerful than we think."

All that was true, and I wasn't going to argue. But there was more.

"The other name for stress-induced cardiomyopathy is 'broken heart syndrome,'" I told Diane slowly. "In other words, I think you can say that your mom died from a broken heart."

There was silence on the other end of the line. "Shit! I love that," she said, her voice catching on her emotions. "Dying from love is so much more meaningful for me than dying from stress."

Her voice broke off again. "They loved each other so much. Mom loved him so much. This is so right. It's so right."

"You and your sister have had it so hard," I said. "Maybe this makes it less hard?"

"It does. And I think we all knew it. I think even Dad knew it—that's why he wanted to stay alive. When we lost one of them, we were going to lose both of them. Even death couldn't keep them apart."

I returned to the more mundane question before us. "So, how do you want me to get these final death certificates to you?"

"I'm going to call Joy. She lives a couple of blocks away. She's off work. Can she pick them up soon?"

Joy came to pick up the death certificates at the funeral home a few hours after I talked to Diane. True to my sense that she was a realist, Joy didn't believe the broken-heart theory. "It feels too much like an ending to a Nicholas Sparks novel," she told me. "I'm not the romantic Diane is."

"I know. It *is* rare," I admitted. "But it makes sense, right? And even if you don't believe it, there's something deeply human about it. Just how connected we are."

"Sure," Joy said. "Just don't let a shitty novelist get ahold of Mom and Dad's story. I don't want it to be sappy. I want the curse words and the hardships, the fights. Their story wasn't so much about romance. But they gave themselves for one another."

—

It took me a couple of weeks to process this whole thing. I see so much interrelatedness at funerals, around death, and in grief. But terms like *community* and *connectedness* have never seemed to capture it.

So I've settled on the term *liminality* to describe what I see. Liminality is the quality of being in a threshold. It's standing with one foot inside and one foot outside, like you're standing right in the doorway of a home. It's the state of being both inside *and* being outside. It's a paradoxical experience in which two seemingly opposing things are both true.

We have a liminal existence when it comes to life and death. Death offers liminal experiences. We like to think that the living are totally alive, and the dead are totally dead. We think that death and life are opposites. You're either dead or you're alive, right?

But it's not like that. It's not like that at all.

When someone dies, part of us dies with them. And even though they're dead, part of them is still alive. Because we are both. The dead are alive in us. And part of our life dies with the dead. We are alive and dead. We are dead and alive.

The dead surround us, live in us, integrate themselves into our soil. We are who we are, we live where we live, we speak the way we speak because of them. Our character is a reflection of theirs because we are them. We are their hopes, their dreams, and their desires.

In an individualistic society, everything is about individual awards, accomplishments, salaries, and possessions. "It's mine because I earned it," "This is who I am," "You do you": such mantras fill our heads.

But we are living cemeteries. We are not entirely our own. We've been carried here—to this moment—by the love, hard work, and heritage of our ancestors. Their love lives in us. Their work carries us. We are theirs. They are ours.

And sometimes when a loved one dies, that loved one is so much a part of us that—like conjoined twins with shared organs—we die too. Literally. It's very, very rare, but it happens. That's what stress-induced cardiomyopathy is.

Any funeral director who's been in the business long enough has likely seen it happen. When it does, it's usually a couple who's been married for a long time and who just can't seem to exist without the other. It's like the couple has become so close that the individuals are conjoined. Some conjoined twin pairs can be separated, although it's a difficult, intricate, and likely painful process. But not all can be separated. Some share vital organs, and the death of one is the death of the other.

We are not just our own. Sometimes we're enmeshed with people who abuse us, and sometimes we're enmeshed with those we love.

I believe that love holds all the mysteries of the universe. It holds the past, the present, and the future. It holds us together, and it evolves us to our higher selves. Love is the magic of the world, but it's more than magic. It flows from the invisible to the visible, from dreams to reality. Love flows from our hearts to our bodies, and from our bodies, it creates the world.

CHAPTER 5

SELVES CONSCIOUS

It was around two in the morning when I googled "stress management therapist near me." I was close to drunk. Funeral directors have minimal opportunity to drink because we're on call so often. I suppose we could drink when we're on call. But what terrible optics for a funeral director to tell a family, "I'm so sorry that your mom just passed. Give me a few hours to sober up from drinking away my existential dread and then I'll be right over."

Alcohol can seem a good substitute for the deep work of self-reflection. Instead of dealing with the pain of this job, many funeral directors take the drunken shortcut to numb their feelings. We're also bad at validating our feelings. It's hard for anyone who works with the dying or the dead—hospice nurses, chaplains, funeral directors—to acknowledge our own pain, as we're constantly helping people in worse pain than we are. We often tell ourselves that our troubles just aren't serious enough to ask for help.

So a lot of us drink. Heavily.

Even though I was drinking at two in the morning, I didn't want to become the stereotype. Google informed me that a handful of local therapists dealt with stress, but only one near me had experience working with all forms of PTSD.

So I emailed that therapist, Peggy, right away, before I lost my nerve. I explained that I was burnt out, depressed, and likely suffering from PTSD due to secondary trauma. Admitting the last item in my list of psychological ills had taken me some time because—like many others—I thought PTSD was only for war vets, abuse survivors, and those who had experienced personal traumatic events. As I'd later find out, PTSD doesn't accurately describe what I was experiencing because my experience wasn't the result of one or two traumatic events. It was cumulative from a continuous barrage of being in the shadow of death.

Over the years, I had become used to my body being in a constant state of hypervigilance. Mostly due to the chaotic and highly emotional nature of the funeral business, I found that every time my cell phone rang when I was on call, I'd go immediately into fight, flight, or freeze mode. I'd answer the phone, talk to the Answering Service for Directors (ASD) call specialist (shout-out to all those wonderful people over at ASD who answer the phone for us during the evenings and nights), and then calm myself down before I called the family of the deceased. Over the years, my body had been slow-cooked in stress and secondary trauma, and I was finally waking up to that fact.

What makes this type of trauma more insidious for those of us who work in deathcare is that while it's continuous and cumulative, it's not directly happening to us. What we experience is called "secondary trauma" (some call it "vicarious trauma"). Secondary trauma is what EMTs, ER staff, police, and, yes, deathcare workers experience when we step into someone else's tragedy. Secondary trauma is never as intense as it is for primary survivors. But over time, secondary trauma can build itself into burnout, compassion fatigue, depression, and even PTSD—all of which I and many others in my profession hide beneath the suits.

Secondary trauma is a quiet trauma—the secret held by caregivers like myself. We often minimize our own pain so that we can focus on the pain of others. Unknowingly and unintentionally, that minimization of our own feelings eventually diminishes our ability to care for those who need us. It also diminishes our ability to care for ourselves.

I guess it's not surprising that we invalidate our own pain through comparing it to others'. This pain comparison hurdle is what we—and men specifically—have to get over before we can find healing. I understand that it's easy to see people who are worse off than we are and altruistically defer attention to them so they can get healed as soon as possible. It's like we do psychological triage in our heads. We see people who are more injured than we are and we let them see the doctor first.

Don't get me wrong; most of the pain we see is worse than ours, but we aren't on a battlefield, and this isn't a war where we're caring for soldiers who have been wounded on the field. If we were in war, we need to see ourselves as part of the medical staff directly assisting the injured. While we may not have the worst injuries, caregivers—like medical staff—are vital for the healing of the wounded. If we don't take care of ourselves, who will take care of the wounded? Too often, we're like the chef who only gives herself the leftovers, the builder whose house is falling apart, the mechanic with the broken car, the parent who goes without sleep. Caregivers are too important to not receive care.

But this isn't war. There are enough resources to go around. The people who really need help can get the help they need and there will still be more than enough help for you, too. We can all get help, and we can all heal faster if we focus on the one soul we can change: our own.

Even though my experiences at the funeral home weren't caused by war, abuse, or violence, I decided that if I wanted to get healthy, I had to do something. I had to validate the vicarious trauma, the traumatic visuals, and the constant hypervigilance that I was unable to navigate on my own.

At the time, my depression was being treated by a smorgasbord of high-dosage antidepressants that I took religiously and that kept me from bottoming out into suicidality. Getting to the point where I acknowledged that I need antidepressants was a journey of slowly unraveling thoughts like: "I don't need help;" "I'll get through this on my own like I always have;" "All I need is for some luck to go my way and this will pass;" "Everybody else has similar struggles and they make it just fine."

It wasn't until I started to see the effects my depression had on Nicki and the kids that I decided it was time. Because for a lot of us, it's easier to care about the pain we're causing others than the pain we're causing ourselves. Over time, I accepted that it was okay for me to get help. The confluence of work hours at the funeral home, my personality, and the darkness of death created a new reality that I wasn't going to get through on my own.

Yet while the antidepressants kept me from hitting rock bottom, they didn't raise my baseline. I wanted something to help me feel more than numb. I wanted to be healthy enough to know joy a few times a week and to be able to handle some of the more difficult emotions like anger and grief without being afraid those emotions might push me toward the abyss.

Peggy's schedule was packed, but eventually she had an opening. Although it was a few months away, I quickly nabbed it.

—

I left my house a little early, as I didn't want to be late to my first therapy appointment with Peggy. Her office was on her home's property. "When you come for your appointment, Google Maps has our address marked on the wrong driveway," her email about the appointment read. "There's a ranch-style house that sits close to the road. That's not us. We're the property with the long drive through the woods. You won't be able to see our house from the road, so look for the house number on our mailbox."

My initial attempt to find the driveway was a failure. I overshot it, turned around, and drove slowly to make sure I found the right mailbox and corresponding driveway. I turned into her lane, and about one hundred feet down the winding drive was a lamppost that looked exactly how I've always imagined the lamppost in *The Lion, the Witch and the Wardrobe*. When Peter, Susan, Edmund, and Lucy walked through the wardrobe and into Narnia, the lamppost welcomed them to an adventure.

As I drove up the lane, I didn't feel any nervous anticipation. I had nothing to be nervous about. I didn't feel shame for my struggles. I didn't feel guilt or condemnation. And I knew that talking about trauma didn't call into question my masculinity. At one point, back when I believed in the idea of original sin—that every human is born sinful and will always be sinful without the imputation of Christ's righteousness (it's confusing, I know)—well, back then I felt like shame was inextricably tied to us simply for being sinfully human. But over the years, I'd come to believe that it's not original sin that permanently impairs; it's original trauma that can be worked through and understood. Unlike original sin, which humans supposedly pass down to each other without fail, trauma doesn't have to get passed on to the next generation. We can break these cycles.

During high school, I led an "accountability group" for my guy friends. We met once a week to talk about our struggles—from romantic confusion to questions about our faith and spirituality. That little group of high school dudes helped me see that vulnerability and transparency aren't weaknesses for men. Vulnerability and transparency are strengths. Becoming aware of toxic masculinity is utterly essential for men. We don't have to hate our manhood—although hating some of the traditional male gender social constructs may be necessary. It just means that men have to realize that thousands of years of evolution have made us aggressive, domineering, and groupish. We no longer live in small huts in the forest where we have to fight off wild animals and defend our families from neighboring groups. That brazen form of masculinity served its purpose in our survival; it helped us reach a place where we can lay it down. Part of laying it down is realizing that puffing out our chests and growling like a bear isn't the ideal of strength.

Peggy wasn't my first therapist. A few years earlier I had met with a therapist named Bruce. The ending of my sessions with Bruce was a case of "it's not you, it's me." I didn't have a framework to see my problem; I could feel it, and I knew it existed, and I knew that it was connected to the funeral home. But my individualistic view of myself kept me from letting Bruce help me figure out what was going on.

Peggy was waiting at the door of her office. She had blonde hair and she dressed like she was comfortable in her own skin. Her hippie-inspired flowery capris and solid blue tunic harkened back to the photos I saw of my parents when they were in high school.

Peggy's office was a detached room that her husband had built for her counseling sessions. There were plenty of windows, some paintings she had done when she was younger, a sofa, her chair, and two little therapy dogs, Dexter and Piper. Her hippie vibe was wrapped in a professional exterior, a graduate degree, and life experience that included living in Turkey and Belgium and eight of the 50 states in America. She had two children, an ex-husband, a second husband, and a grandchild on the way.

I had no intention of laying everything out in the open on my first session. Instead, I prodded a bit, seeing if I could chip away at her professionalism and the academy behind it. I wanted to know the real Peggy. I think I wanted to know how she'd treat some of my very tender spots if I showed them to her.

Good therapy is a process that helps us see ourselves for who we are. Each session you show up with fewer and fewer psychological clothes. Most of us are afraid to show our naked selves. We put layer after layer of clothing around our hearts so that no one sees the embarrassing parts. Good therapy is the process of psychological and sometimes spiritual undressing—and hopefully finally realizing that there are no "embarrassing parts."

In our first session, Peggy told me, "I'm never going to tell you what to do. I want to give you confidence in yourself to make your own decisions."

That statement, which seems so basic and obvious, was exactly what I needed to hear as I began therapy. While my grandparents and parents had told me that I could do anything I wanted, I always felt like anything other than being a funeral director just wasn't in the cards. The confidence that I'd been given was that I'd make a good funeral director. Despite the lip service given to the idea that I could do anything I wanted to with my life, my parents had the same narrative ingrained in them by their parents and grandparents.

It wasn't just my family that pointed me down this journey, I told Peggy. "Numerous people have told us they're glad the Wildes will bury them," I said. "That just reinforces the narrative we've been told time and time again. If I didn't become a funeral director and stay one until I retire, I'd not only be letting down my ancestors; I'd be letting down the whole community."

For most of my life, the narrative that I was given was that my confidence was tied not to my own gifts but to my family's history and my part in that history. I wasn't sure who I'd be if I separated myself from that history.

"So what do you think would happen if you left the funeral home?" Peggy asked.

"I think I'd feel better about life," I said. "But I've been told that it's not just about me. In fact, I've been suicidal a few times, and a few times I've nearly acted on it. But each time I came back to work as soon as I could."

I went back to work because, well, that's just what we do at Wildes. We show up, no matter how we're feeling.

—

My ancestors were exceptional at reading people's expressions. We trained our brains to see and identify people's needs, emotions, and desires on a professional level. We're so good at it that we've been paid to do it for 170 years. That's my ancestral inheritance.

As a writer, I'm never going to be the type of writer whose style and content are an amalgamation of the 150 books I've read over the past year. I'm the type of writer whose style and content are the amalgamation of the 150 families I've walked with through the valley of the shadow of death.

My heritage has less "book smarts" than it does "people smarts." So, my dear reader, I'm sure a few typos have made it into this book. Believe me when I say that it's not my editor's fault. When you consider the amount of typos she had to deal with, you'd expect one or two to slip through the cracks.

People smarts can help in life, but they don't always help in school. I was the one who saw the kid crying on the playground. I saw the ones who were lonely, the ones who were angry, the ones who were broken. (I had a more difficult time seeing math problems. And an even harder time seeing math answers.)

Why could I see some things and not others? I suppose it's because of my ancestors. Back then, I didn't understand why I noticed the emotions of my classmates while many of my friends seemed immune to others' feelings. If I hadn't joined the funeral home and watched how my dad relates to grieving families—if I hadn't seen how my grandfather notices the same things that I've noticed—I might have just thought I was weird. Even though I was wondering now if I was cut out to be a funeral director, I realized that working at the funeral home had helped me see the world the way I do.

"I'm not just me," I explained to Peggy. "Self-sufficiency was never stressed upon my mind. I was constantly told that I could be the sixth generation of Wilde funeral directors— and the continuation of funeral directors on my mom's side of the family. I'm not an isolated individual who can dream his own dreams, plan his own plans, and be whoever he wants to be."

That seemed to make sense to Peggy. "So maybe your problems aren't just your problems," Peggy suggested. "Maybe your trauma isn't just from your own experiences. Maybe you're here, right now, with me, because you're carrying the dreams of your ancestors."

We sat in silence for a bit, and then she continued. "I think you also carry their trauma," she concluded. "It's going to be helpful, as we continue this journey, to recognize your heritage. You aren't just carrying your own hopes, dreams, and pains. You're carrying the entire six generations of the Wildes and five generations of the Browns."

The critic in me wanted to dismantle her logic. It's obvious that my feelings are my feelings alone, right? This idea—that I was somehow wrestling with the shortcomings or emotions of my ancestors—infringed on my individualism, and I didn't like it. The critic in me wanted to say that the foundation of personhood is to believe that I am an individual. After all, we don't punish the children for the sins of their fathers and mothers. We are each responsible for our own actions.

But despite my internal arguments, I knew she was right. I am not on my own. My grandparents and great-grandparents and great-great-grandparents—and on back—were still speaking. Through me.

"It's not going to be easy unpacking everything, Caleb," she said. "Because there are things that you hold that are larger than you. That's why you have such big feelings. They're not just your feelings. You're feeling the feelings of multitudes. If it were just you, you'd likely be able to wrestle though your thoughts on your own."

"It's not just *you* living inside your body," Peggy added. "And when we start to unpack the things we're going to unpack, you won't just be unpacking your own baggage; you'll be unpacking generational baggage. And hopefully, at some point, we can do more than unpack their baggage for them. Hopefully, we can give fresh life to their hopes and dreams."

CHAPTER 6

A SMALL PART OF
A BIGGER STORY

Reconnecting with our ancestors isn't always easy. You may find yourself part of a story that's shameful and possibly even evil. Maybe your family never had the privilege of a recorded history, or maybe your ancestors had their history erased by oppression. Like me, you may find yourself part of a story laden with expectations and responsibility.

Most of our ancestors were carried along by systems and people more powerful than themselves. Despite their importance to us and our lives, most of our ancestors can't be found in the stories of written or oral history. Usually they weren't the ones creating the historical shifts. They were the ones being shifted.

In 1851, the first generation of Wilde funeral directors played a role—an insignificant role, but a role nonetheless—in an event that would unintentionally lead to the birthing of the funeral industry in America. Although our small part is historically negligible, it's more than significant for me. This story still shapes the almost mythical narrative surrounding my family's funeral home. It is why I have often felt strong-armed by my ancestors, both alive and dead, to lay my dreams at the altar of the family business. This story is what Peggy was helping me uncover in our sessions.

Here is the tale of the event that led to the event that led to the funeral industry. It's an industry that has supported six generations of Wilde funeral directors. To tell one story, I have to tell another—because stories, like people, are all connected.

—

William Parker was born in 1822 on the Roedown Plantation in Maryland. The son of Louisa Simms, an enslaved Black woman, Parker wasn't entirely sure of the exact date he was born. The plantation owner kept better records of his cattle, Parker noted, than of the people he enslaved.

When William was seventeen years old, he fell sick and didn't feel healthy enough to work. "Master Mack," the plantation owner, noted William's absence in the field, and he told William that if he didn't start working, he'd be whipped. William refused to work, and when Mack came to fulfill his threat, William managed to grab the whip away from him and beat the slaveholder.

Knowing the retaliation would likely be deadly, William fled north to seek his freedom. He made his way some twenty miles north of the Mason-Dixon Line and ended up in Christiana, Pennsylvania. Christiana is in Lancaster County, and it's the town where my mother grew up. William began farming land just a few miles from my home in Parkesburg.

The area surrounding Christiana had more than a few fugitive-slave catchers, the most notorious of which was the local Gap Gang. Slave catchers would storm into a house late at night or early in the morning and snatch a freedom seeker. Then they'd hustle them back to their enslavers, often beaten and bruised, to collect their reward.

William became a member of the Lancaster Black Self-Preservation Society, a network of freedom seekers and allies with eyes and ears and guns on the lookout for bounty-motivated "fugitive catchers." On one occasion a local girl was kidnapped, causing the preservation society to spring into action. They retrieved the young girl, but not before William got shot in the leg. He would later cut the bullet out with a penknife. Such stories meant William Parker developed a reputation for being a badass freedom fighter.

Despite constant threats, William stayed in Christiana, married another freedom seeker, and had children. He lived a relatively happy life—until everything changed in an instant on September 11, 1851.

Two years prior to that fateful day, four enslaved men—George Hammond, Joshua Hammond, Nelson Ford, and Noah Buley—had been charged with stealing wheat from their slaveholder, Edward Gorsuch. They fled the Maryland plantation and ended up in Christiana, where William Parker connected them with work.

As part of the Missouri Compromise of 1850 between the slave states and free states, a stricter Fugitive Slave Act was put in place. Edward Gorsuch had been trying to find a legal way to reclaim his "property" for two years when the Fugitive Slave Act opened the door for him. Gorsuch went through the state and federal legal avenues and thought that he could, through kindness and forgiveness of the supposed thievery, convince the "fugitives" to come back to his farm.

Word had spread throughout the Christiana community that Gorsuch and a search party were in the area, seeking to capture the four men. Gorsuch led a group that included his son Dickinson, a US marshal named Henry Kline—to prove the legality of the whole thing—and an assortment of friends and family.

Although William himself laughed off the rumors that Gorsuch was in the area, two of the freedom seekers that Gorsuch was after decided to stay at William's home, where they would be safer.

At around five o'clock on the misty morning of September 11, Gorsuch's group arrived at William's home. One of men that Gorsuch had enslaved had just left William's house and was on his way to work when he saw the group arrive. He ran back to the house to warn the others. Gorsuch's men gave chase, and although they didn't catch him, they managed to get through the front door. They stood inside the door while he ran upstairs to alert all the others.

William, aware of what was happening, came halfway down the stairs to confront the intruders. "Who are you?" he asked.

Kline spoke up. "I am a United States marshal," he said, the full weight of federal law enforcement in his words.

I can imagine the tension. On the first floor stood a group of white people, armed and utterly convinced of their righteousness, bent on capturing Black people and returning them to enslavement. The second floor held a group of frightened, angry, and armed free Black men and women.

In the middle of it all stood William Parker.

"If you come any closer, I'll break your neck," William told Kline.

Kline showed his identification and repeated his demands. He explained that he and Edward Gorsuch had legal authority from the US government to procure four pieces of Gorsuch's property.

Undaunted, William chided, "I don't care for you or for the United States government."

William believed that once a "slave" set foot in a free state, that term was replaced by the title "freeman." So he answered truthfully: "Anyway, there aren't any slaves on this property," he concluded.

At this point Gorsuch intervened, telling William he was going to go up to the second floor. "I'll go and get my property," he said. "What's in my way? The law is in my favor."

With a strength and confidence that likely shook Gorsuch to the core, William told Gorsuch that he'd be in grave danger if he came any closer.

Was it the tone of William's voice that changed his mind? The stories he'd heard about William's unflinching courage? In any case, Gorsuch changed his strategy and had his men leave the house and stand outside the front door. Instead of going into the house, he called each of his former enslaved men by name and told them that they were coming with him. He told them that he'd treat them kindly and that he'd forgive them for stealing his wheat.

But, as William said, there were no slaves in that house anymore. There was no one to obey Gorsuch's commands.

Marshal Kline, rebuffed by William's firmness, threatened to burn the house down. William called Kline's bluff and replied, "You can burn us, but you can't take us."

While this was going on downstairs, William's wife opened the second-story window and sounded a horn that let all the neighbors know they were in danger. While she was leaning out the window, one of Gorsuch's men fired a shot at her. It missed, and she ducked behind the window and kept blowing her horn. Over the next few minutes, a couple of shots were fired from William's home, all missing their targets who, at this point, had vacated Willliam's home.

William pulled his gun, shot, and just missed Gorsuch's head.

Amazingly, tempers calmed down for the moment, the two groups collected themselves, and Gorsuch spoke directly to William through the open front door, with William still standing his ground in the house.

Realizing that civil law didn't have the kind of authority he needed to win, Gorsuch started to appeal to a higher power by quoting scripture at William Parker.

William responded in kind, forcefully quoting so many scripture verses that Gorsuch was surprised at how much he knew about the Bible. William concluded his argument by asking Gorsuch, "Where do you see it in scripture that a man should traffic in his brother's blood?"

Gorsuch understood the aim of William's question and responded, "Do you call a (Black person) my brother?"

William's reply was simple and final. "Yes."

It is said that Gorsuch lowered his head but said nothing.

After the scripture volley was over, William shouted, "Go home, old man. Go home before you get hurt." Gorsuch dug in, telling William he wouldn't leave until he got his.

Soon, thirty-five freemen and freewomen came running to the aid of William Parker, carrying clubs, stones, guns, pitchforks, and corn cutters. Additional white men showed up as well—some saw themselves as "fugitive catchers," and others were neighbors concerned for William and his family.

One white man named Castner Hanway was commanded to assist Gorsuch and responded, "You have come to the wrong place for assistance. That, my conscience will not permit me to do. Negros are no property and have the right to defend themselves."

Hanway and another white, Elijah Lewis, tried to get Gorsuch to leave, to no avail. Sensing what was to come, Dickinson Gorsuch also begged his father to leave. After two hours of back and forth, the lines had been drawn, through politics, scripture, and words. There was nothing left but action.

Some of Gorsuch's party began to back off, including Edward Gorsuch himself. It was said, however, that immediately before the fight, Edward turned toward William's house and said, "My property is here, and I will have it or perish in the attempt."

Although the accounts vary, the chaos started when Edward Gorsuch was struck with a club. Dickinson rushed to his father with pistol raised, but he was struck down with club and bullet before he could reach him. The remaining members of Gorsuch's group started to fire on William's people, but the bullets largely missed their mark. Frightened and outnumbered, Marshal Kline retreated. The gravely wounded Dickinson Gorsuch was dragged out of the fray. Everyone but Edward Gorsuch followed.

Edward Gorsuch was dead.

William Parker would later say that Samuel Thompson, one of the men formerly enslaved by Gorsuch, "struck him the first and second blows; then three or four sprang upon him, and when he became helpless left him to pursue others."

Finishing his retelling, William emphasized that it was the women of the group who put an end to him.

—

A couple of years before the Christiana Resistance, Isaac Wilde, my great-great-great-grandfather, emigrated with his mother from Ashton-under-Lyne, Lancashire, England. He jumped around a couple of jobs until he ended up working at a cabinetry shop in Atglen, Pennsylvania, roughly two miles away from Christiana. At first Isaac worked with a friend named David Moore, but by the time 1851 rolled around, Isaac had taken over the cabinetry shop in Atglen.

There wasn't a funeral industry in 1851. There weren't any funeral homes or licensed funeral directors. Embalming was only being used for scientific purposes, as a way to preserve cadavers for dissection and medical education. There were hardly any metal caskets, and few if any cemeteries required burial vaults, as is custom today. Cremation was still viewed as a pagan practice and wouldn't even take place on US soil until 1876, when Dr. Julius LeMoyne built a crematorium in Washington, Pennsylvania. Funerals, viewings, and burial were tasked to the church community and family and friends.

The coffins were made of wood and were placed directly in the ground. The earth took back the casket and the unembalmed body, resulting in what we now call a "green burial."

There were, however, coffin makers who would help with funerals. Most of those carpenters who made coffins weren't making coffins as a full-time job; they were cabinetry shop owners who, in addition to chairs and cupboards and beds, also made coffins. Isaac Wilde was one such undertaker, the first of what is now six generations of Wilde funeral directors. At the time, Isaac was the only carpenter in the Atglen and Christiana area.

By evening, Gorsuch's group had collected his body and taken it back to a hotel in Christiana. Marshal Kline got a message to Isaac Wilde and had him make a coffin and a shroud. Isaac had little time to build the casket, and he enlisted a young boy to help him build Gorsuch's coffin.

Isaac likely took the coffin to Gorsuch's men by placing it in a wagon, harnessing his horse, and going up and over Zion Hill, a small community that still houses the descendants of the freemen and freewomen of the Christiana Resistance. There was likely ice lining the bed of the coffin to slow the decomposition of Gorsuch's body. The following morning Gorsuch was shipped back by train to his home near Baltimore, Maryland, while his son Dickinson lay, gravely wounded, in the home of a local Christiana Quaker family.

At that time, Atglen and Christiana held a significant population of Quakers, who were well-known abolitionists and participants in the Underground Railroad. They were one of the main reasons men and women fleeing slavery came to Christiana and Atglen. David Moore, Isaac's original business partner, was a Quaker. Isaac's daughter and son would eventually marry Quakers. And Isaac also came from England, where slavery was outlawed in 1833.

I don't know why Isaac chose to settle in an area that had strong abolitionist roots, whether it was for practical reasons or because it gelled with his personal beliefs. I do know that Isaac started a relationship with the Zion Hill community.

Wilde Funeral Home still serves the descendants of the Christiana Resistance who live on Zion Hill and worship at the Mt. Zion AME Church, a church commissioned by Bishop Richard Allen in 1817.

But in 1851, white people in the American South felt no love for the Christiana Resistance. The reaction was immediate and violent. More than six thousand people took to the streets of Baltimore to protest. A myriad of southern newspapers decried the "injustice," labeling it the "Christiana Riot." Today, many whites still call it the "Christiana Riot," a term that favors the slaveholders. Bands of roving bounty hunters from the South ravaged the surrounding Black and Quaker homes, on the lookout for the escaped William Parker and his friends. They broke into homes, overturned furniture, and kidnapped anyone who fought back. Claiming the resisters were "runaways," they used violence to procure information on the whereabouts of William and anyone else involved in the resistance. The bounty hunters even came to the Mt. Zion AME Church building and shot through the front door to gain entrance. That door is currently on display at the church as a reminder that Mt. Zion AME overcame persecution and survives to this day.

On September 13, Marshal Kline named and charged fifteen Black people and two whites with "aiding and abetting in the murder of Edward Gorsuch." Since William Parker and many of the key players couldn't be found, the two white men, Castner Hanway and Elijah Lewis, found themselves at the center of the trial.

When they surrendered to Kline, he reportedly got in their faces and shouted, "You white-livered scoundrels, you, yesterday, when I pled for my life like a dog and begged you not to let the blacks fire upon us, you turned round and told them to do so." Lewis denied Kline's claim. Hanway did not deny it and was charged with five counts of treason.

The trial became something much larger than the resistance itself. It was a battle of power on a national scale. Abolitionist lawyers took up Hanway and Lewis's defense. The judge framed the trial in favor of Hanway, and the jury found him not guilty. As a result of Hanway's trial, all of the charges against the other resisters were dismissed. US Marshal Kline was later indicted for lying in court.

The resistance, in conjunction with the verdict, utterly incensed white citizens in the South, who considered the trial a joke. Some historians have suggested that the Christiana Resistance could be considered the first battle of the Civil War.

William Parker, his family, and some of the other key participants of the resistance fled to New York through the Underground Railroad. They went all the way to Rochester, where Parker connected with Frederick Douglass. Douglass himself would later say that the Christiana Resistance, along with John Brown's raid, was one of the major harbingers of the Civil War.

Without the Christiana Resistance, I don't know that the funeral industry would exist. Without this event, I don't know that I would exist.

What happened next in this story changed a nation. And it changed the way a nation cared for their dead.

—

So the Christiana Resistance would help spark the Civil War. Embalming would first be used for restorative purposes during the Civil War. An estimated forty thousand of the six hundred and fifty thousand soldiers who died in the Civil War were embalmed. But if there was a single event—a single death that created some form of traumatic bonding to embalming in the psyche of Americans—it was a death closely related to the Christiana Resistance.

At the time of Edward Gorsuch's death, one of Gorsuch's sons lived at a boarding school with his longtime friend and schoolmate, John Wilkes Booth. Booth and Gorsuch's son would remain close until Booth's assassination of Abraham Lincoln in 1865. Booth's brother promptly destroyed most of Booth's writings and belongings after he assassinated the president, but a letter remained. It was a rough draft of Booth's manifesto, an explanation as to the reasons behind his action. In that letter, Booth recounts the impact that Edward Gorsuch's death had on him and how the unresolved injustice done to Gorsuch needed retribution.

Lincoln's body was embalmed by Civil War embalmers Drs. Brown and Alexander (who had also embalmed Lincoln's young son, Willie Lincoln, in 1863). A train carrying his embalmed body traveled around the northern states, making stops in twelve major cities. It's estimated that a few million people viewed the train and participated in the viewing of Lincoln's embalmed corpse as it traveled over 1,654 miles. More than any single event, this stamped the value of embalming on the minds and hearts of the American people.

My mom, her parents, and her two sisters lived in the Brown Funeral Home in Christiana, a funeral home founded in the early 1890s by my great-great-grandfather William H. Brown. Mom would have been the fourth generation of funeral directors in the Brown family had she been given the choice to join it and accepted that invitation—although she now works at the funeral home as our secretary, so she is a deathcare worker and very good one at that. Some four miles east of Christiana lived my dad, his parents, and his two sisters at their family-owned Wilde Funeral Home in Parkesburg.

So as I've said before, I'm the product of two separate funeral directing families, and it's pretty fair to say that if the funeral industry didn't exist, my grandparents, my aunts, my cousins, my parents, my sisters, and I wouldn't exist. Both funeral homes started out as furniture shops, and if it weren't for the Civil War and the advent of embalming in the United States, their furniture shops would have only lasted until the industrialization of furniture. Then their lives would have splintered off in different directions, likely never connecting.

More than forty thousand Civil War soldiers were embalmed. Abraham Lincoln's embalmed body was viewed by mourning Americans as it traveled by train through the northern states. As embalming became imprinted on a mourning nation's psyche, the funeral industry was born, eventually becoming a multibillion-dollar profession. The splintered ripples of those events ping-ponged to 1981 when I was born, bringing along with me out of the womb the expectation that I'd take my place as the sixth generation of Wilde funeral directors.

My generation was told we could be anyone we wanted to be. Each of us was unique, we were told, and each of us had unique dreams. Our individuality and uniqueness were underscored and underscored and underscored. To be happy, we were told that we must understand our individuality and purpose, and we must claim the dreams that are uniquely our own. We were told that our dreams, our goals, and our paths are valued over the dreams, goals, and paths of our family and community.

I, however, was given a different story than my peers. I was born with the dreams of my ancestors attached to me, to fulfill my place in a long line of funeral directors. For me and my progenitors, the funeral home and its continuation have been more important than our individual dreams.

The deeper that therapy with Peggy and research into my ancestors' lives took me, however, the less sure I was that the funeral industry was right for me.

That's right. In a statement that constituted family heresy, I wasn't sure I belonged in this line of work. It was heresy because the very thought of it could destroy a linage that was created by generations of hard work, resilience, and community investment.

If I left the family business, was I selfishly discarding everything my ancestors had invested in me? If I left the business, would I be putting my own needs above the business and our community? At this point in my life, though, I wasn't sure I'd be leaving to pursue my own dreams. I'd be leaving because I wasn't sure if I could handle death anymore.

CHAPTER 7

THE BEGINNING
IS LISTENING

The Mt. Zion AME Church congregation shows more affection toward us Wilde funeral directors than any other church we serve. Don't get me wrong; the other local churches give us a lot of love too. So many generous churches await us on those days we hold funerals in their places of worship with hugs and—even more important—a fresh pot of coffee. Mt. Zion, though, not only gives us coffee; they always send us home with plates of home-cooked food.

I was sixteen years old when I first worked a funeral at Mt. Zion AME Church. And I was nervous because I could imagine what my whiteness meant to those attending the funeral. By the time I was sixteen, I had already been to countries where I was a minority. The previous summer, I had lived among the Mixtec people of the state of Oaxaca in Mexico for a few days with a host family. While my host family treated me well, the other people in the village were unwelcoming, even spitting in my direction and kicking pebbles at me as I walked past them on a pebble road. The rejection and language isolation (my host family spoke no English and I only spoke a little Spanish) kept me on the brink of tears during the entirety of my stay.

At the time, I hadn't understood how imperialistic and violent the United States had been to the Mexican people. At one time, what is now Texas, California, Nevada, most of Arizona, half of New Mexico, and parts of Colorado and Wyoming were part of a young and newly independent country of Mexico. When the United States took those parts of Mexico, we did so by killing five thousand untrained Mexican troops (the US lost seventeen hundred soldiers), and four thousand Mexican civilians.

When enough of us white people go anywhere, our history gives pretty good evidence that we're planning to just take over (see: white people history in North, Central, and South America, all of Africa, and a significant part of Asia). My skin and nationality carried the violence inflicted by my ancestors on the Mexican people from more than 150 years earlier. When I entered the Mixtec village, people didn't just see a fifteen-year-old American, they also saw my ancestors.

So over the years I was learning, slowly, that I wasn't just "Caleb Wilde." I was also a part of a people who had inflicted violence on anyone who got in our way. Even though I thought I was a "good person," I knew that I carried a lot with me whenever I walked into a Mixtec village or an AME congregation. Not only did I carry with me white ancestors who had hurt others, but I also carried centuries of privileged assumptions that made me racist in ways I wasn't aware.

When I walked into Mt. Zion AME Church in Atglen at the age of sixteen, I knew what my skin represented. And because of that, I wasn't sure that I could serve Mt. Zion well. I wasn't sure that Black descendants of the Christiana Resistance wanted me to serve them. I mean, if the tables were turned, I'm not sure I could trust the people who built a coffin for Edward Gorsuch.

Beyond that fact, being a funeral director for a family involves a deep level of trust. In normal seasons of life, people often shrink themselves around other people. We defer and tiptoe and act polite. At a funeral and around death, the real self comes out. The real person. Death makes us all psychologically and spiritually naked. Vulnerable. From what I've been told and from what I know, people of color often find, in routine daily life, that they have to shrink themselves around white people. And grief should never be shrunk, and funeral rituals shouldn't either. I feared that my presence would be detrimental to their grief—diminish it, somehow.

At sixteen, I had only attended white funerals. White funerals are subdued, mainly because we like our rituals to be like the god we've created: unemotional, disconnected. Public emotion is not only seen as a weakness for white people; it's scarier than a gallon of skim milk a day after its expiration date. We're afraid of grief. Then again, maybe we're right to be scared. White grief, white anger, white grievance, white fear: sometimes racialized emotion seems so close to the surface, and we subconsciously and consciously know how horrible it can be when we let it out.

The phrase "celebration of life" that's found its way into so many obituaries underscores the sentiment and takes it a step further. Now we're not only privatizing our grief, but we're saying that public emotion is only acceptable if it's painted with a smile. It's a beautiful thing to celebrate a person's life, to be thankful for all the goodness and love they've created in the world. But there's no need to further shame our grief by telling mourners that—in the words of many of my white friends—"good vibes only" are welcome at funerals. There's no shame in public displays of grief. It's okay to be sad. It's okay to grieve, both in private and in public. But, as a young white boy, I had only seen private grief.

Before I went to my first Mt. Zion funeral, Dad told me that the funeral would be different from those I had experienced in the mostly white churches surrounding us. He was right.

First: us white people in the Parkesburg area—and, I suspect, in most areas of the United States—come early to a viewing. Because that's what you do for white people viewings. You come early and greet the family of the deceased so that you beat the line of other white people who are thinking the exact same thing. All the "avoid the rush" people arrive in the first half hour of the viewing, thus creating the rush they were trying to avoid. White people hate waiting in line almost as much we hate uncontrolled display of emotions. And waiting in line while there's an actual dead body to be viewed? Torturous. Before attending a viewing, white people will often say to each other, "I just want to get it over with."

That's not how it works with the AME viewings, at least in our area. The family always arrives a few minutes before the funeral service starts. And there's rarely a receiving line. If you're there for the viewing and you arrive before the family, you just walk up to the casket, take a minute or two, and then leave if you're going to leave. Otherwise, if you're staying for the service, you grab a seat in the church.

So when a white coworker, neighbor, or friend who has come super early sees that there's no receiving line for the viewing, they usually look to me, as their fellow white person, and ask, "Um, is the family here yet?" When I tell them the family will arrive right before the funeral service starts, they'll grab a seat and wait for the family to come.

But then the family doesn't come the way the white friend expected. They expected that the family would come and that there'd be a chance to quickly shake hands with the family members they know so they can get back home and mow the lawn. They didn't expect that the family comes to the viewing all at once and all together, fifty or sixty people strong, making a procession from the back of the church to the casket. And they didn't expect the whole group to be led to the casket by the pastor, who is speaking out scripture verses of comfort.

So there we white people are, sitting in the pew, getting a small taste of what it feels like to be a minority. Up to now, the white person's patience may have been slightly tested. But as the preacher leads the family past the casket, white comfort is about to be tested. At this point, the white people often see something that makes them uncomfortable: a public display of grief. For white people, grief is almost always a private emotion. There are incredibly few situations in which a white person would feel comfortable expressing an intense emotion in a public setting—usually involving sports, games, or gender reveal parties. But definitely not funerals.

White people might express grief in private, but even then they rarely talk about it. At funerals I've seen in AME churches, there's screaming, there's anger, there's tears, and there's fist pounding. Some attenders are overcome by emotion and collapse, all while family and friends are calling out the name of the deceased.

It's nearly impossible for humans to understand difference if we only hang around our own people. We become so accustomed to the way we do church, the way we do ethics, the way we do food, the way we discipline our children, and the way we do relationships that seeing a different way of doing life—and death—can seem so very foreign. We all get used to our own ways and have difficulty understanding the ways of others. But when the "we" is referring to people of privilege, what is "different" is often somehow "wrong." Because privileged people have the privilege of believing their way is the right way without it being questioned.

So when a white person sits through a Black funeral and sees a very different way of dealing with death, that discomfort often makes us think, consciously or subconsciously, that the Black people are doing this wrong. "This service is taking too long," "There's no chance for me to give my condolences to the family!" and "That's not the Holy Ghost I'm used to."

But if the white person sticks around and tries to receive with an open heart, they may find themselves in the presence of those who have gone before. They may find themselves witnessing a spirituality of the hereafter they didn't even know they were missing.

—

The idea of connecting with ancestors transcends cultures and times. Those of us from European heritage have been disconnected from the concept of ancestors' presence. This has happened through Protestantism and, as I'll talk about in a moment, the Enlightenment. The idea of past generations being a part of our spirituality might seem jolting to white people. But as civil rights activist Ruby Sales suggests, there's a "spiritual crisis in white America." Sales calls it "a crisis of meaning." I wonder whether white people's disconnection from past generations is one aspect of this spiritual void in the lives of white people.

White people shouldn't appropriate the way other cultures connect with their ancestors. We shouldn't make other cultural practices our own. But we can learn from them, and when we see those rituals in action, they can give life to the ancient embers that we have tamped down.

In my experience, white funerals only conjure the living. White people are even fond of saying, "Funerals are for the living." Occasionally, there will be a white funeral in which it feels like the family and friends conjure the dead person to participate. These funerals usually include a "sharing time," in which the family and friends share such clear stories about their loved ones that, for a moment, it's like the deceased has walked into the room, poured a cup of coffee, and sat down.

Sometimes even I, as the funeral director listening in, feel like I'm meeting the dead.

When the people at Mt. Zion sing during a funeral service, it feels to me like they're inviting all generations of their ancestors to join. The family and friends of the deceased aren't just reconnecting to their ancestors through the hymns. They're letting out generational grief that comes from a thousand voices. It's as though their ancestors join in the grief of the loss. For AME families, funerals are not just for the living.

My European ancestors set the individual mind as the primary feature that makes humans, well, human. We thought that the mind and the way we use it is what sets us apart from animals, and so it stands out prominently in European history. Descartes's "I think, therefore I am" sums up one of the building blocks of European and American civilization. There's no "we" or plurality in this building block. This isn't a plural "you." And there's no reference to how feeling or relationships makes us human. That's all left out.

It might help to see how individualistic the "I think, therefore I am" statement is by contrasting it with something more communal, such as: "We love, therefore we are." Or the southern African concept of *Ubuntu*, "I am because we are."

When Descartes first wrote the phrase "I think, therefore I am" back in 1637, he likely didn't see some of the consequences that "I" and "think" would have on cultures that place high value on community and connection. People of privilege can easily heap scorn upon cultures that value community and connection because privileged people see their supposed self-sufficiency as superior, even though that "self-sufficiency" is actually sustained by those they oppress.

If we redefine "I think, therefore I am" to something like "I'm connected to others, therefore I am," it changes how we view those who come before us. We no longer see them as totally dead and living in the hereafter, but as a part of the here and now, in life and in death.

Telling white people that we're a privileged group fights against our "pull myself up by my bootstraps" interpretation of our life's narrative. It calls into question our identity as "I." If the work and effort that "I" as an individual made ends up being a corporate and communal effort, white people feel like their value is being called into question. We white people have believed the lie that to be somebody, we have to make ourselves better. If we believed that our value is derived by making communities better, we would likely have an entirely different world.

In other words, those who live within a culture of community and connection—those who see the self as plural and not singular—smack against our pride. Humility for white people starts with acknowledging how dependent we are on community, on our ancestors, and on others for all that we have. It's sitting down at our dinner table and acknowledging that the meal we're about to eat was only cooked by us, while the ingredients were packaged by others, grown by others, raised by others—and not just by people, but by the earth, by creatures that we sacrificed for our livelihood, and by the dirt of decomposed life. Nothing we do is just our own. Until we lose our pride and find humility, we'll never be able to step outside our own skin in self-reflection and see our own whiteness.

And we can do it. If white people have something going for us, it's that we're stubborn as hell. We just have to get

stubborn in the right spaces and about the right things: fighting for criminal justice reform, working for equity, advocat-
ing for policies that level the playing field, and fighting for
reparations. Because Black ancestors' lives matter too.

When we begin to listen to all the ways our dead still
speak, we begin to fill a void we may not have even noticed.
We may not like what we discover, but this is the hard work
that needs to be accomplished to move forward. When we
understand our collective past, we can change not only the
future for our descendants, but we can take our ancestors
with us.

—

So much of the world's pain over the past couple of centuries
has come from the hands of those who spoke my language,
whose history I share, whose skin I wear, whose politics,
laws, power, exploitation, and murder I benefit from to this
very day. I sit on the shoulders of a giant who stands on a
mountain made of exploitation and the dead bodies of those
who stood in our way.

I am ashamed to think that my ancestors were a part of
such hatred and inhumanity. As a white person trying to
reconnect with my ancestors—both those that I'm directly
related to and those with whom I'm connected through
race—I'm not so sure I want to. Honoring them, in light of
the hatred and pain they gave to other human beings, doesn't
seem right. Yet if connecting with our ancestors, and allowing our dead to speak, sits so fundamentally at the core of our
spirituality, we must find a way to connect. It is a hard truth.

For me, understanding the plural self helps me grasp my responsibility as a white person with a clearer mind. If I realize that my cluelessness about the white supremacy I benefit from isn't just my personal problem but something that's been passed down, I can approach the work in my own life without being overwhelmed by guilt and shame. Dr. Ibram X. Kendi's definition of antiracist—"one who is supporting an antiracist policy through their actions or expressing an antiracist idea"—has also helped me move beyond my "surely not me" reaction to racism. Racism is everywhere. It's in our ancestors, in our communities, and in ourselves. White people can't be "not racist." At our best, we're humbly identifying racism in ourselves and in systems and actively working against it.

Most of our transgressions in our personal lives are individual in nature, and so is the apology. If I do something wrong to Nicki, I own my shit, ask her for forgiveness, and ask her what I can do in the future to repair the wrong. That's on an individual level. And I, as an individual, do my best to be humble enough to admit my wrongs. In communal cultures, with plural selves, there's another level to that process.

Christianity claims that God is a plural self: that God is three in one. Perhaps the three-in-one trinitarian view of God acts as the template for how we can understand ourselves. If we're made in God's image, we can't think of ourselves in any other way than a plural self: interconnected to those we love in the present as well as those we love in the past and the future. Some people talk about the trinity like it's some mystery of the Christian faith. But it's only a mystery for people who see individualism in everything they look at. Is God one person or three persons? The answer is yes. It's the same in you and it's the same in me. Are you one person or many? Yes. You are the one and the many.

When I was nineteen years old, I traveled to Madagascar with a missions team that did both Christian things and humanitarian things, like trekking medical supplies into remote villages. We were there for a month. A couple of days into our trip, our team went to a remote village where, some fifty years earlier, a majority of the village population was murdered by the French military. Madagascar was annexed by France in 1896, and in 1947, a Malagasy revolution began against France. Madagascar won their independence from France in 1960, but not before the deaths of more than eleven thousand Malagasy at the hands of the French army.

The organization we worked with had driven us out to see a communal reconciliation meeting between some French humanitarian workers and the leaders of this particular Malagasy village. The humanitarian workers began their involvement in the village by first acknowledging their ancestors' wrongdoing. When we arrived, the residents of the village had gathered for this meeting, encircling the French humanitarian workers, who stood together. Across from them, on the other side, stood the Malagasy leaders of the community.

Once the meeting began, the French read about the atrocities their army had committed in the 1950s. They then walked over to the Malagasy leaders, got on their knees, and asked forgiveness for the brutal deaths committed by their people. The Malagasy leaders accepted, lifting the French from their knees and embracing them as a sign of forgiveness. Then the French stayed and gave resources to the tribe—not as wealthy benefactors assuaging the guilt of excessive privilege but as people making an incredibly small effort towards the sweeping reparations that need to take place on a global scale.

Although I felt the power of this repentance ritual, I had a hard time understanding the whole thing. At that time, I had such an individual view of wrongs, apologies, forgiveness, equality, and justice. These particular French people had not themselves brutally murdered the people in this village. These French humanitarian workers were here to help, to give of themselves, their time, and their resources. And most of the Malagasies who stood across from the French were likely not even alive when the murders occurred. But when the French workers and the village leaders hugged, both sides were reduced to tears.

Communal sins need communal confession, communal forgiveness, communal restoration, and communal justice. The individual self has a hard time grasping this. But when we deepen our understanding of the plural self—that is, the me that is not separate from the groups to which I belong—it begins to make a whole lot of sense.

I remember Peggy's words in our first therapy session. "You're carrying the entire six generations of the Wildes and five generations of the Browns," she told me then. "It's not going to be easy unpacking everything, because there are things that you hold that are larger than you."

I am writing this while looking out into the night sky. I am thinking about what the night sky has seen as it has looked at humans for the past three hundred thousand years. It has

seen so much unspeakable injustice, unspeakable pain, so
much sickness, loneliness, and selfishness.

The sky has seen it all.

—

We bring our ancestors with us. Although we can work for
repair and reparation, white people can't ever fully repay for
our actions done to people of color. These horrors can never
be undone.

But to hold onto hope in this world, I have to believe that
a new view of the self, not as a singular but as plural, might
be possible. I hold onto hope that with every step I take—
toward listening, toward humility, toward repair—I bring
my ancestors with me. If their acts are in some way mine,
then perhaps my acts are theirs too. When I embrace, they
embrace with me. When I listen, I make them listen too.
Perhaps we honor our ancestors by becoming our best self
and by amplifying the best in others.

Bringing our ancestors with us doesn't atone for their acts
of hatred. But I wonder if, in the afterlife, they have now
seen their sins, confronted their evil. Perhaps they're calling
on us to make sure we don't repeat them. It's easy to think
of our ancestors as behind us, but I'd like to think they're in
front of us too. Some of our ancestors might still be calling
us backward. I imagine there are some who are still stuck
in hubris and still demanding we restore the old, harmful
ways. But what if most of them are in front of us, guiding us
forward? I'd like to think that whatever it is inside of us that

calls us forward is more than just our consciences. I'd like to think it's their voices too.

And if our ancestors are calling us to repair, perhaps one day we will join them. We will become ancestors too, cheering our children's children with every step they take toward justice and equality. Our best hope is that if we carry our ancestors, our descendants will carry us too—toward a future reality that now only exists in our imagination.

CHAPTER 8

BRINGING MY ANCESTORS WITH ME

I woke up at 6:30 a.m. to a radiant winter morning. The snow had been predicted to come during the witching hour, and by the time morning came around, the small storm system had already left. The morning sky was blue, and the earth was white with the kind of snow that stuck heavily to the naked trees, roofs, and ground. The clear Pennsylvania sky and winter air allowed the sun to bounce its undiluted rays off the new snow, creating a morning that demanded sunglasses.

I took a quick shower, dug out the old black suit that I use specifically for mornings like this, put on my black winter boots, and grabbed my worn wool trench coat. Throwing my thirty-inch snow shovel in the bed of my plow truck, I slushed off to the funeral home, where the snow-covered driveway and sidewalks needed to be cleared for a morning funeral.

It was a rushed morning. I usually like to take my time when I wake up. Normally, I sit down on our living room couch and surf news sites as I drink a blended glass of banana, almond milk, and vegan protein powder. Then it's a ten-minute shower, during which I plan out the coming day in my head and take a few

minutes to meditate. On days that I have a funeral, I take my
time picking out my suit, making my best attempt to match
my shirt and tie with my various hand-me-down cufflinks
and tie clips. I do my hair. Spray some of Tom Ford's Oud
Wood on my suit, take my thyroid pill and antidepressants,
and head to work. But when I wake up to a surprise over-
night snow, that routine gets cut down to a quick shower
and a smoothie without the news.

As I drove down Main Street toward the funeral home,
I passed by Pop-Pop's house and saw him sitting in his
enclosed porch across the street from the funeral home. His
fixed gaze followed me as I plowed, shoveled, and salted the
driveway and sidewalks. After I had finished the funeral
home, I started shoveling his sidewalk, working my way up
to his front porch, where he greeted me with a "Thank you,
Calebee." He invited me into his enclosed porch, which was
surprisingly warm thanks to the small heater.

"You sure you want to stay in this business?" he asked, rec-
ognizing that I looked worn down. He'd asked me that same
question many times before.

When I first started working at the funeral home at age
sixteen, Pop-Pop had me follow him around as an appren-
tice. He was so proud to introduce me to Parkesburg people
as "the sixth generation of Wilde funeral directors." Time
and time again, he'd tell people that I was the "next generation of Wildes." He would say it with such genuine joy that
I felt important and needed. His pride in what I represented
was contagious. For a time, his joy was my joy.

What made me feel even more proud of my heritage in the
Parkesburg community was the way people would respond

after my grandfather introduced me. They'd give me a look like I had just been accepted into their family. Men would reach out a hand for me to shake, and women would give me a heartfelt hug. Because I was a Wilde and was going to be a funeral director, they loved me. It is an amazing thing for a young person to feel so genuinely accepted into a community. All the love that my family had given to the people of Parkesburg was reflected back on me, and it made me feel like I was special.

After I got my funeral directing license, Pop-Pop was even more of a herald of my arrival. Before I became a funeral director, he'd introduce me to his friends; after I became one, he'd introduce me to anyone who happened to be nearby. He loved having me by his side. And for the first fifteen years of working full time at the funeral home, I was always by Pop-Pop's side. He would eventually start calling me his "right-hand," both a compliment and a statement of respect.

Yet his respect wasn't easy to earn, even as a grandson. While he was more flexible than many funeral directors, he had high standards and expected everyone who worked with him to meet them. The catch is that those standards were rarely ever communicated—at least verbally. Funeral directors become experts at reading nonverbal communication because grief has a way of bungling up the connection between the mind and the mouth. But even though the mouth might not say what people want, there's other cues we can pick up on. A widow rarely tells us that she wants to spend a couple of extra minutes alone with her deceased husband before we make the removal from their home. But we can tell by the way she's fixed her eyes on his face that she's not ready. The deceased's children don't tell us they want to walk with us as we carry their parent from the house to our removal van, but I can tell by their body language that they don't want to leave their dad's side. These are just two examples, but the reality is that many people don't know what to do when they've just experienced a loss. Part of my job is to put words to their feelings.

I'm good at it too. Reading people is my real-life superpower. But there's a shadow side to that superpower, and it's a shadow side that my family of funeral directors—and I imagine many others like us—have experienced. We become so good at reading other people's nonverbal cues that we start to expect our loved ones to do the same to us. We fall into this trap of believing our attention to nonverbal cues helps us mind read; and if we can do it, our loved ones should be able to do the same to us. This can have devastating effects on a marriage, on friendships, and on parenting. See, Pop-Pop loved the fact that I read his nonverbal cues so well, and that's why he started calling me his "right-hand"—and not his "right-hand man," mind you, but his own right *hand*: an extension of his own thoughts and intentions.

He also grew to respect my personal work ethic and my perspectives. He started to let me make decisions about technological upgrades, such as the funeral home's website and various other improvements. He'd commission me to take on difficult projects, like tracking old insurance policies that families would dump in our laps or drafting legal letters or spearheading the funeral home's change from a partnership to an LLC. Not only did I have my Pop-Pop's love as his grandson and mind reader, but I had also come to earn his respect. I began to feel like maybe I was supposed to be a funeral director after all. If Pop-Pop thought I belonged here, maybe I did.

So there was a time that I could answer Pop-Pop's "You sure you want to stay in this business?" in the affirmative. But now, after years of slowly realizing that I couldn't continue to handle the work schedule and seemingly limitless secondary trauma, well, on this day I lied to him.

"Sure," I said in a reassuring voice, trying to compensate for my banal word choice. I knew what I represented to Pop-Pop. I was his future. I was the funeral home's future. And that question wasn't meant to give me an opening to say no. It was meant to give me another chance to reaffirm my commitment to the family business.

I was afraid to tell him the truth: that I was burned out and depressed. I was afraid to tell him that I didn't think I was cut out for this work after all.

Later, I would tell him as much. In the midst of the pandemic that was to come, I was so burned out that I didn't have any leftover filter to purify my true thoughts and feelings. I'd tell him that I thought the funeral home had caused significant damage to our family's communication skills and that the funeral home had damaged his relationships with his family.

But that truth telling was still far off in my journey toward reconciliation with my ancestors. Today, I didn't want to tell him the truth because I didn't want him to doubt the stability of his lifelong legacy that had been passed down for me to carry. I didn't want to tell him that the legacy was too heavy and that I was ready to set it down. I wanted him to take joy in me like he had when he was introducing me to people.

I knew that the stories he had told himself weren't even his own stories. The story had gained steam as the fifth and sixth generation of Wildes entered the business, but even as the fourth generation of Wilde funeral directors, I'm sure Pop-Pop was celebrated just like I was by both his family and the community. I'm sure that he felt like he was carrying a legacy. And unlike me, he had fought hard for this business, invested in its growth, and saw his struggles turn to success.

I knew, though, that before I could tell Pop-Pop the truth of what I felt, I needed to go back even further, to the beginning of the narrative as it formed and grew in the lives of my ancestors.

By 8:30 a.m. the sun had worked in tandem with the salt and cleared the driveway and sidewalks of all the snow. And it was just in time, as a sudden influx of family cars started pulling into our parking lot. Everyone expects to be directed into their proper place in the funeral procession car lineup. After the funeral is over, and we start our procession to the cemetery, the spouse of the deceased is the first in the car lineup. Spouses always go first—unless there was some marital or family friction, in which case spouses sometimes don't want to be first. And then the kids are next, usually in order of age. Then the siblings of the deceased, followed by other nonimmediate family members. This particular family was large: five adult children of the deceased, all in separate cars. Six siblings, all in separate cars. Most of the time, the family cars come in intervals, but this morning they all came at once.

I was standing in the parking lot, frantically waving my arms like the marshallers at the airport as they're waving directions to the pilots. "You go here," I mouthed, pointing emphatically to the parking spot designed for child number three. "You, here," I said, making direct eye contact with another driver. "A little more. A little more." Slowly we got the cars inched in as tightly as possible to make the most of the limited space our parking lot provides.

While those fifteen minutes of high-level Tetris were stressful, the nice thing was that once those cars were parked, I had all the family in place. By the time the last family car was parked in the parking lot, I had a good forty-five minutes of attending to the parking lot with minimal work before the official start time of the public viewing. I had our lead car running with the heat on full blast, so I could catch a break from the cold, and a few minutes before the service began, I jumped in the car and decided to start my reconciliation with my ancestors by texting Celeste.

—

After Gerda and I had talked about having a small funeral for Noshi, she planned a service for Noshi and invited a few family members and friends to her house. Gerda asked Chaplain Celeste from hospice if she'd be willing to give the eulogy, and Celeste obliged, with a eulogy that focused on how we can celebrate overcoming the second death by keeping our loved one alive in our hearts.

After Noshi's funeral and Chaplain Celeste's eulogy, I wanted to be Celeste's friend. Before I left Gerda's house, I sought Celeste out and chatted with her about her job and mine. We talked about Mt. Zion AME Church and all the scars on the stairway walls from caskets being hoisted by

pallbearers up and around the tight-but-still-doable turn
from the stairway into the church's sanctuary. We exchanged
cell numbers and said the frequent polite (but often dishonest), "Let's do coffee sometime!"

Today, from the warmth of the car in the parking lot, I
texted her. "If you have some time, I'd like to do coffee and
talk about ancestors," I texted.

"How about today?" she replied.

"You sure?!? I got a funeral til noon. Can do my lunch
break at one."

"Perfect. At Dunkins?"

"See you there."

By 1:00 p.m. I was sitting across from Celeste with my coffee and she with hers. She had just finished visiting a string
of hospice patients. We traded some stories about our jobs
for a few minutes before I popped the question.

"Celeste, do you think we can speak to our ancestors?"

"First off," she started, "while I like using the term 'saints'
instead of 'ancestors,' I think we mean the same thing. Second, let's not limit our conversations with our ancestors to
just speaking."

Cultures produced by the Enlightenment are convinced
that our mediums of communication—writing, storytell-
ing, and oral history—are *the* best way to communicate, she
said. We've believed in those mediums because the Enlightenment says that our emotions, even our thoughts, are just
mental states.

Unlike our mind-centric forms of communication in the
West, she said, other cultures, especially African tribes,
"speak" through dance. Each movement in each dance has

a meaning. It speaks of tribal values, of love, of wisdom. It's embodied, nondualistic sacred text. It's embodied text that spans generations. "When these cultures dance, they're conversing with their ancestors, who danced the exact same dance in the same way from generations back," she said.

Celeste explained how experiencing love or grief is not just a mind experience; it's an embodied experience. She said she hears grieving people say all the time, "I just don't have words for what I'm experiencing." She tells them it's because grief is not just words; it's mind, heart, hands, and feet that grieve. We need to find avenues to let all of our body grieve— and maybe then we can find some words.

"To get to your original question," she said with a smile, "it's unhealthy to pathologize conversing with our ancestors. There's a fear that talking with our dead leads to some sort of idolization of the deceased and pulls our attention away from worshipping God."

"That's why Protestantism did away with icons, right?" I asked. "Didn't they think that venerating icons was the same as worshipping idols? It's like there's fear that if we get too close to anything but God that it's somehow idolization."

"The pathologizing of communicating with ancestors is a part of colonization," Celeste pointed out. "If colonizers can control the ancestors, they can control the living. It's the politics of death. It's sad, Caleb, but this idea that communicating with ancestors is wrong is a broad stroke from Protestants and evangelicals."

She knew that much of my hang-up with conversing with the dead was because of my evangelical background, and so she took her talking points in that direction.

"Conversation with the dead isn't the same as worshipping them. We're talking right now, and you're not worshipping me! Now, if you want to worship me by giving me all your possessions, I'm not *opposed* to that," she said with a snicker.

"Even reverence for the dead isn't the same as worshipping them," she went on. "A codependent relationship with our ancestors is different. Believing that every act, every plan needs to have the ancestors' stamp of approval: that isn't growth. Both God and our ancestors want you to become your own person, just the way you want to see your boys become their own person. You're raising them to be independent adults, not dependent children who need your affirmation at every turn of their lives."

She paused, and we sat in silence for a moment. "Our good ancestors empower us. That's what a saint is. We all have saints in our family. Sometimes we have to look a little hard to find them, but they are the ones we need to focus on, because when we do, we touch a generational power that travels from the past to the present."

Her eyes focused right on me. "Caleb," she continued, "we draw strength from each other in life, we're empowered by each other in life, and we're protected by each other in life. Why can't we also be strengthened, empowered, and protected by both those alive and dead?"

—

A few days later, I found myself in my therapist's office, telling Peggy about my conversation with Pop-Pop. "When he asked me if I wanted to stay in the funeral business, I lied to him by telling him yes," I told her. "He has put so much of his life's work into the funeral home, and he is so proud knowing that I'll carry on that work."

I paused. "There's this heaviness in me whenever I say that out loud," I said. "There's a heaviness that I didn't place on myself. It's heaviness from my ancestors, who I feel are none too pleased with me ending my part of their legacy. And all this heaviness, this whole narrative, is represented in my Pop-Pop."

I told Peggy I felt like I needed to address my ancestors before I addressed Pop-Pop. I wasn't sure why I felt that way, but it seemed that he was just one of many generations of funeral directors on both my paternal and maternal sides who saw me as their legacy.

Peggy listened, and as my summary of my dilemma came to a close, she asked, "So do you want to speak to your ancestors about what you're feeling?"

Talking to the dead sounds odd, even to me. In my work I do talk to dead bodies, but I think many deathcare workers do that, to personalize the dead. It's therapeutic to humanize our jobs, and carrying on a one-way conversation with a dead body makes it feel like more than just flesh. But talking to disembodied dead people? That was something psychics and mediums did, not funeral directors. My inner skeptic started spewing out all the reasons such a conversation is just imaginary, a coping mechanism to deal with my feelings of insecurity about leaving the funeral home.

But Peggy was just asking me to remember: to take what I knew and felt about my ancestors and to interact with those feelings in a meditative sort of way. I laid down on Peggy's therapist couch, covered myself from head to toe with a blanket to give myself a feeling of safety, and tried to calm the skeptical voice inside me as Peggy guided me to think about some helpful prompts. After I felt calm and safe, I started.

"So, um … well, listen: you all have worked so hard to make me who I am," I said out loud. That way Peggy could also hear my thoughts and redirect me if I went off on a tangent. "You all created the opportunity for me to live, and I'm thankful I've got to experience sunsets, mountains, and love. I know I represent so many things to you. Yes, I'm your descendant, but I also embody all the hope that your work will continue on beyond you. I'm it. Both sides of you, the Browns and the Wildes, know that I'm the one to keep the funeral directing tradition in our family lineage. I'm aware that I'm the culmination of your hard work, pride, and sacrifice."

I paused and opened one eye, and Peggy gave me an encouraging nod. "But, um, I want you all to know that I'm not on earth to keep your names alive or be your flag bearer. And I'm not going to pressure my children to enter funeral service. I know you all love me. And you should be proud of who I am. All the love you've poured into me—I'm using all of it. I'm using it for good. I'm helping people. I have a wonderful, healthy marriage. By all accounts, I'm a good father."

I took a deep breath and kept going. "You all know you were broken, right? You all know that it's not healthy to see as many dead children as you all have seen? It distorts a person to see so much grief and pain. You know this business may sharpen our compassion, but it also deadens so many other things. I know you all harbored anger. I know you all suffered from secondary trauma. I know this because it's in my genes. I feel the anger and trauma deep inside of my bones. I know some of you had terrible marriages. I know some of you weren't great parents. I know that some of you were not as Christian as you pretended to be."

The longer I talked to them, the easier it became. I imagined them sitting on a bench in front of me, hands folded in their laps and expectant expressions on their faces. "I know you all meant well by grooming me to be a funeral director. Mamaw and Pop-Pop, you've told me, 'It's a respectable job' at least one hundred times. You're right. It is a respectable job. But I'm not sure if I'll ever be the funeral director you want. I am your legacy. But I'm your legacy in love, not business. Every good thing you've done that has passed to me, I'm passing it on to my wife, to my kids, and to myself."

I quieted myself for a few moments and then said just a few more words. "I will honor you all. But not in the way you all want me to."

I kept my eyes closed for another minute or so. Whether imagined or not, I felt them respond. And in that moment, I knew it was time to leave the funeral home. I knew that I was free to go. "We love you," I heard them say. "You are who we hoped for. And we're proud to be your ancestors. We just want to come with you wherever you go."

CHAPTER 9

HE CAME TO ME THE OTHER NIGHT

Gerda and I had been meeting for coffee semiregularly. We usually picked a corner table in Dunkin' Donuts. The corner table in any coffee shop is the table that says, "I don't want to be bothered." It's the table the introverts grab, and it's also the table that hears the deep, vulnerable stories and feelings. Sitting there, you can feel somewhat hidden—if hidden is even a thing at a coffee shop. Over those months, Gerda had told me her story.

When Gerda met Noshi, she wasn't just a student at Heidelberg University; she had declared herself an orphan. Her dad, Hans, had lost his father in World War I, leaving young Hans to fend for his mother and three of his younger siblings. With the combination of a father lost to war, and the Depression that followed in Germany, Hans's angst and anger found a home in the nationalism of Nazism and a fervent commitment to the Third Reich. After fighting in and surviving World War II, Hans was left even more bitter and disillusioned than he was before it began. His abuse and latent nationalism scarred Gerda's youth, so she decided to escape through the ladder of a university education at Heidelberg.

"Leaving home was the most difficult choice I've ever made," she told me. "I left two young sisters at home with Hans [she refused to call him Dad] and Mom. He abused me, and Mom did nothing to stop him. But I was okay with his abuse as long it wasn't aimed at my sisters. You can find deep resilience when you know your pain is protecting someone you love."

Gerda told me she knew that if she left, that abuse would probably go to someone else, like one of her sisters. She decided to go to university for a year and see what happened. If Hans started abusing her sisters, she thought, she'd go home. But if he didn't—if her father managed to conquer his demons—she'd stay. That was her plan.

And then she met Noshi at a bar. Noshi was a kind, shy soul, but he gave her plenty of signals that he liked her. Gerda wasn't sure she liked him. He was American. An American soldier. Dating him was sacrilege to many German men and women. I guess it'd be similar optics if a young American woman started dating someone from the Taliban right after 9/11.

For Germans in the early 1950s, the word "Nazi" didn't carry the same connotation that it carries today. Our fathers, our brothers, our uncles who fought in the war were just cogs in the system, or so we thought. They were just nationalists who wanted to restore national pride.

"Even after the war, many thought that Nazism was a good idea that was poorly executed. The Allies weren't the heroes we know them as today. They were the ones who put a stop to our nationalistic hopes and dreams. And being the slightly rebellious girl that I am, I liked that I was dating one. At first,

I think I dated Noshi to spite Hans. I wanted Hans to know that I was dating a US soldier. I wanted him to know that I wanted nothing to do with him or his dreams."

"Well played," I said with a smirk. "Did your dad ever end up abusing your sisters?"

"No. He started abusing my mother. My sisters blamed me for it all. And they haven't talked to me since Heidelberg. I don't know if they're dead or alive. I know Hans and my mom died in the 1980s. My aunt got ahold of me and told me. Frankly, the world is better off without him."

"Good Lord," I said. I told her I thought she should provide the listener a shot of whisky before she told them her life story. At least some wine.

"Oh, Caleb," she said. "But Noshi! My rebelliousness and spite for Hans gave me Noshi. Noshi and I never needed each other. We've never been dependent on one another. Both of us are ferociously independent. We weren't two separate puzzle pieces that completed each other. Our relationship began because Noshi was nice and I was rebellious. Over the years, we loved each other. There's no magic. We weren't 'meant for each other.' We just *became* each other. And as we grew older, we were each other's company.

She smiled. "The older I've become, the more I've loved Noshi, not for who he is, but for who we can be when we're together. We kept each other from being lonely and gave each other enough smiles and good conversation to make life good. We never aimed for perfect."

Gerda's voice sharpened a bit. "Noshi and Hans are complete opposites. I hate Hans for all that he was. I hate my mom for letting things happen. They are, Caleb, the deepest, loneliest, most bitter part of my person. The part of me that is my parents is a part of me that's full of painful memories and death. It's a part of me that feels dead. Completely dead."

We sat quietly together for a moment. Then I spoke. "I have a story for you," I said. "I'm not trying to force you to do anything. You have every right to hold your parents accountable for what they did to you. I guess this story is interesting because it addresses that part of you that is completely dead."

Anytime she wanted me to stop telling this story, I said, I would stop. This story was hard and macabre and horrific.

—

A week earlier Dave Farve, the Chester County deputy coroner, had called the funeral home with a death call.

"You know Jerry Roberts?" he asked me.

"Jerry used to work at St. John's Cemetery. Larger guy with a Santa beard, right?" I replied.

"Yeah, that's him," Dave replied. "Except he's likely larger than the last time you saw him. He's been sitting in his unair-conditioned apartment for over a week. Bring the gloves and your shit clothes.'"

Every summer brings with it a decomposing body or two. They're special cases, special in all the wrong ways. Dad and I loaded up the removal van, grabbed some aprons that we usually use for embalming, a thick plastic body bag that we call a "disaster pouch," and begrudgingly sped off to meet Dave in Jerry's apartment.

Jerry lived in a four-story apartment complex in Coatesville—an apartment complex that on this day had an inoperable elevator. This wouldn't have been a problem if Jerry hadn't died in his third-floor apartment. We carried the removal cot up the three flights of steps, and as we entered the third-floor hallway, the smell hit us.

A decomposing human body is an especially repugnant smell. I had to stuff my mouth with Altoids, a strategy that sometimes manages to mask the smell. Not this time. What had made matters worse for the entire third floor is that someone had opened the windows and door in Jerry's apartment, giving the wind opportunity to blow the decomposition smell out the front door of his apartment and into the apartments of all his neighbors.

The neighbors had discovered Jerry's death in the first place, so I assumed they were somewhat used to the *eau de Jerry*. Discovering a decomposing neighbor in an apartment building usually begins with folks wondering if maybe a mouse has died in the wall. The next level of questioning is something like, "Did the cat die and we didn't realize it?" Sometimes people wonder if the sewage is backing up somewhere. And the last question asked is, "Has anyone seen Jerry lately?"

The neighbors then call the apartment manager to check on Jerry, and the manager calls 911. Soon after that the coroner arrives, and then that's when we show up, in our outfits that look like space suits.

Jerry was slumped over in his recliner. There were half-eaten TV dinners and newspaper sections spread throughout the room. As I looked around, it wasn't just the dinners and newspapers but everything in the house that was placed at random around the room—except for one thing. A neatly stacked pile of *Playboys* sat beside his chair.

When I'm in a conversational setting and the topic moves to stories like Jerry's, I usually preface the story by giving my listeners an opt out. I'll say something like, "I can give as much or as little detail as possible. If anything grosses you out, let me know and I'll stop." I'd done that with Gerda, and she was encouraging me to keep going. But let me break the fourth wall at this point and advise you to skip the next couple of paragraphs if you fall on the "as little detail as possible" side of spectrum.

Jerry's face was reddish blue, and his lips were a solid blue. His tongue was swollen so that it was protruding out of his mouth, and some of the stomach juices had worked their way up and bubbled out of the sides of his mouth.

All that type of thing is fine for us funeral directors. Really. But what's difficult for us is the skin slip that affects a decomposing body. *Desquamation* is the technical term, but *skin slip* describes the actual problem a whole lot better. When you go to grab a decomposing corpse's arms, or legs, the skin often slides off the deceased, creating a less-than-desirable concoction of human fluid. On a thin person, you can usually find ways to control the skin slip, but on a guy like Jerry, where you're just grasping for a grip, you're glad you wore the shit clothes like the coroner told you to.

What makes decomposing bodies like this especially sad is that there's usually a reason the body hasn't been discovered earlier. That is, the deceased hadn't had anyone checking in on them. True, some people just like to keep to themselves. But others are lonely souls who have burned bridges along the way.

A few days later, when Jerry's eighty-something-year-old mom, Patricia, and his son, J. J., who was a couple of years older than me, came into the funeral home to make arrangements, I quickly sensed that Jerry's case was the latter.

J. J.'s body language clearly said, "I don't want to be here." But it wasn't because he thought funeral homes were scary or that he had to take off work to be here. It was body language that said, "I don't want to be here because I don't like my dad." Honestly, I was surprised he even came. Throughout the arrangements he sat stone-faced—until we started to talk about the obituary.

I asked him what he'd like to say. He finally looked at me and said, "Nothing. I don't want an obituary for him."

His grandmother reached for his hand, and he pulled it away. She tried to say something to him, but he quickly cut her off with a quivering voice and said, "He doesn't deserve it. Not after what he's done to us."

I found out later that Jerry was an addict—an addict who had used up until the last five or six years of his life. He had tried to reconcile with his son, but J. J. would have nothing of it. Jerry had been addicted to meth.

At this point in my story, Gerda jumped in. "Methamphetamine! You know that's partly responsible for turning my dad into a devil. The Nazis gave it out to all the soldiers during the war to give them more stamina and less fear. It was called

Pervitin. My dad was addicted to it during the war, and when he came back home, he used alcohol to compensate for the withdrawal. The first week he was back, he broke my mother's arm and bruised me all over my body."

She told me that Noshi had friends who had used methamphetamines during the war. Essentially, she said, the Nazi *blitzkrieg* was fueled by meth. The soldiers were required to take it. The term *blitzed* actually comes from that drug-fueled initial push by the *Wehrmacht* into Europe, she said.

"I probably would have used drugs too," I said to Gerda. "I'm not sure if a fully conscious mind can handle war."

"Back to the story," Gerda urged.

So at the funeral home, after Jerry's son, J. J., had reaffirmed that he didn't want an obituary for his dad, Jerry's elderly mother, Patricia, stared at me with an expression I could only interpret as indifference. It's hard seeing an eighty-year-old woman indifferent toward her dead son. I've seen children hate their dead parents, I told Gerda, but I had never seen a parent indifferent toward their dead child.

But I thought that Patricia must still have *some* love for Jerry. For all his faults. All the sleepless nights he must have caused her. All the times addiction hurt her and her family. I don't know exactly what happens to love when somebody is an addict. Maybe it becomes like an unwatered and wilted plant, clinging to the hope of rain. I'd like to believe that even though Patricia seemed indifferent, there were memories of Jerry as a child that gave her a sense of joy and love.

J. J. came back the same morning I met with Gerda for coffee, to pick up his dad's cremated remains. I hadn't been sure that he'd ever pick up the remains, I told Gerda. We have about thirty boxes of unclaimed cremated remains at our funeral home. Some of those remains haven't been claimed because the next-of-kin say that it's just too emotionally difficult to figure out what to do with them. But a larger number of those unclaimed remains are there because the deceased was so alienated from family and friends that no one wants them. The family has abandoned the deceased probably because the deceased abandoned them. They sit waiting, in our closet, just in case a family member remembers and decides it's time for the remains to come home.

But that morning, when J. J. came in to pick up his father's remains, he came in with a different countenance. He didn't have the "I hate everyone" look on his face. It seemed like some burden had been lifted, a burden he'd been carrying for far too long.

He came in with questions too. He asked first if I thought his dad had suffered when he died. I was honest with him. "It looks like he died from a 'widow-maker' heart attack,'" I said. He asked me what that was and why I thought his dad died from it.

"Well," I told him, "your dad died in his chair, and as far as I could tell there wasn't … a physical struggle."

J. J. asked for more, so I explained. "Well, if he had felt the heart attack coming, he probably would have gotten up, and we would have found him on the floor, or most likely in the bathroom. But he was just there. In his chair."

"If you don't mind me asking," he implored, "did it look like he was eating? Did he have a book or a magazine in his lap?"

I stammered around a bit, but he cut right to the chase. "Was it *Playboy*? Was he looking at *Playboy*?" he asked.

Half relieved that I didn't have to be the one to tell him, I told him that it was. "Did the coroner tell you?" I asked.

"No. Dad did," he said simply. "In a dream I had the other day. I had a dream that Dad told me what he was doing when he died. We had a laugh about it because he loved *Playboy*, and I guess he died happy. After we laughed, he asked me for forgiveness. Then the dream stopped."

J. J. continued. "When your dad called me yesterday and told me that Dad was ready for pickup, for the first time in decades I was ready to bring him into my home. He was a part of me that I had abandoned years ago. He was a part of me that was dead. It's weird, but now that my dad's *really* dead, it feels like he's back in my life. I had damned him to hell, and now … I don't know, it's like I've found peace with him.'"

I wasn't surprised by his dream. Few things surprise me anymore. Even though I doubt more than half the things that I hear, I've heard them enough to start believing they're real, actual things that people experience. And I told J. J. that—that I believe him.

Cremated remains are about the weight of a gallon of milk. They're not heavy, but I nevertheless usually offer to carry the remains to the car. I made that offer to J. J. He took a moment, a moment that I would guess was used to think about what he should do. After a few seconds, he reached down and picked up his dad's remains. "I'll carry him," he told me as walked out of the funeral home.

—

Gerda looked at me across the table in the donut shop and said, "I don't like that story."

I apologized. I didn't mean it as prescriptive at all, I said, but I told it simply because it was relatable to her situation.

"I don't like it because some people don't deserve forgiveness."

I decided that our relationship was strong enough that I could probe a bit. "Can I ask your permission to explain to me what Hans did that's unforgivable?" I asked. "Again, I'm not trying to judge how you feel. I'm trying to understand how you feel."

"You have my permission, and that's a good question," she said. "I don't have a reason, I suppose."

I quickly interjected and let her know she didn't have to have a reason.

After a moment of thought, she said, "I mean there's not just one reason."

"Oh, okay," I said. "So there are multiple reasons."

"Yes. There are multiple reasons. But honestly, it's just how I feel. I want his memory dead. I don't want earth to remember him."

Gerda continued. "This is a topic that many modern people wrestle with. How do we understand and accept our grandparents when we find out they were racists? Or what happens when we find out that dead author whose books we love to read was homophobic?"

Gerda's questions made me think. I, for one, sure don't want the future to judge me by its standards. It's possible, for example, that in the future we'll recognize the sentience of animals to the point that eating animals will be considered a crime. Do I believe that eating animals is criminal now? No. Is it causing pain? Yes. But many people today either haven't been presented with better options, or they simply don't have better options than meat for protein. Certainly, the vegans of today will be praised by the vegans of tomorrow for their early adaptation and their leadership in taking the world away from meat. But can I judge my ancestors by tomorrow's standards, when meat was a vital way that enabled them and their children to survive?

"Look," Gerda was saying, "wrongdoing assumes you have the ability and knowledge to do what is right. Most people long ago had the same loves as you and me. They wanted to provide for their children and their families and their friends. When they were given better ways to do that, they changed. Many traditional Christian mothers who find out their sons are gay, for example, are finding that love is the way forward, not hate. Acceptance and not exclusion. Why? Because love has a way of winning over time."

Since that conversation, I've kept thinking about how much we want future generations to assume the best of us. We want them to assume that we genuinely wanted goodness. We want them to assume that we genuinely would change if presented with a better way. We want them to assume that we did the best with what we were given.

Human history is messy. Our descendants won't be able to remove themselves from their ancestors any more than we can. But we can change. And if we change, we're changing our ancestors too. We're in this together. You can't separate the human from human history. When we decide to become better, more compassionate, more equitable people, we bring our ancestors along with us. When we decide that an old perspective is wrong and exchange it for another, we bring our ancestors along with us. When we decide to break a generational cycle, our ancestors are empowering us to lift the hammer.

Future generations will certainly see things we did wrong. When they can chart a better way, I, for one, will lend them my full support. If they need to tear down something I built so that they can reach the next level, they have all my love and all my permission. Because I'm going to assume the best in them. I'm going to assume that if they're tearing down something I built, it's for the better. I'm going to assume that if they call out something in me that I unknowingly did wrong, it's for the better for their children and their children's children. I'm going to assume that, just like me, they will be looking out for the best for themselves and those who come after them.

I said something like that in my conversation with Gerda now. "When the future looks back at me and sees my flaws, I'm going to assume, that despite my imperfections, that I and those who come after me share the same heart for a better world," I said, putting down my coffee cup. "I'm going to believe the best of future generations, and I ask that they believe the best of me."

"Yes, I agree," Gerda said and then paused. "But I can't forgive what Hans did. He would never see the mistake in his ways. If his soul lives on, I think it lives on in the same bitterness and hatred he had in life. I see no path forward. I'm glad he's dead, and I don't like talking about him because I want his memory to die with me. I want all of him dead."

Just as she said that, Pop-Pop walked over to our corner table. He was a regular at Dunkin' Donuts, usually grabbing his small coffee with cream and two sugars and whatever donut suited his tastes that particular day.

"Who do you want dead?" Pop-Pop chuckled as he came over to say hello.

"My father," Gerda replied.

"He's still alive?" Pop-Pop asked.

"Oh, no. He's been dead for a while. I want his *memory* dead," Gerda told him. "That's why I'm not forgiving him. I figure if I don't forgive him, he won't continue on in me."

In a moment of rare self-reflection, Pop-Pop told Gerda that he's not too good at forgiveness either.

"It's not that forgiving people comes hard to me," Gerda replied. "It's that I feel like forgiveness gives my father a space in my life, and I don't want him to have that space."

CHAPTER 10

DIRTY HEAVEN

There are only a few green cemeteries in the eastern part of Pennsylvania, none of which are close to our funeral home. Green Meadow Cemetery, some two hours' drive away in Lehigh Valley, appeared to be the closest. I called the contact number at the cemetery, and a woman's pleasant voice answered. "Hello," she said cheerfully. It seemed as though I had called someone's home telephone number.

"Hi. My name is Caleb," I started. "Is Ed available?"

"One minute," she replied. Soon, Ed, the name attached to the website's contact number, had grabbed the phone and introduced himself. We chatted for fifteen minutes or so about Green Meadow and the philosophy behind it. I explained that I was interested in what he was doing and wanted to see the green cemetery firsthand.

I asked, "How's this coming Thursday look?"

"I have a doctor's appointment in the morning. Thursday afternoon is clear. Say, two?" Ed replied.

"I'll see you then."

I asked Ed to meet on a Thursday because I knew both Celeste and Gerda were available to come with me. A few years had passed since I had first met them, and the world was just starting to hear about the coronavirus. Like most people born and raised outside of the United States, Gerda was well aware of world news. She told me how quickly it was spreading in other countries and that the United States wasn't taking it seriously enough.

Having said that, Gerda wasn't taking it too seriously either. Gerda had been diagnosed with inoperable glioblastoma, and her doctor had told her that she'd have around a year to live.

"Death by COVID is probably a better way to go than brain cancer," she told me.

That's why we were going to Green Meadows. She was planning her funeral and was excited about the prospects of a green burial.

I picked her and Celeste up in the funeral home's Escalade, and we started on the two-hour drive up to Bethlehem, Pennsylvania. Celeste jumped in the back because she had some phone calls to make, and Gerda rode shotgun.

"Why green burial?" I prodded, knowing that her husband, Noshi, had been cremated and assuming she'd follow suit.

"I love the idea of it," Gerda began. "Think about how lovely it is that the earth takes us back into itself. It's like we're crawling back into the womb and awaiting to be transformed into the grass and trees. The earth welcomes our body back to itself and repurposes and reuses what it had given us at birth."

"Isn't it weird," she continued, "that so many people have been embalmed? It's like they're rejecting their mother by attempting to keep their body out of her care for as long as possible. I don't know what to compare that selfishness to—maybe it's like a person who takes all the dinner scraps and keeps them away from their dog until they're unusable."

"I'm not afraid to admit that I'm just dirt," Gerda reasoned. "That's okay if I'm just dirt. I don't need to live forever to feel good about my life."

Gerda started seesawing each sentence back and forth as she belted out her extemporaneous afterlife manifesto. "I don't need eternal life as a reward for good deeds. I don't need eternal life to help me make sense of death. I don't need eternal life to have my loved ones with me. I don't need eternal life as a counterweight to all the evil happening now."

And then she went on another tangent, as she was prone to do. "Death helps me value the moment. Death helps me fight for justice in this life, because this one is it. Death and its finality help me see miracles every day. Because it's utterly amazing that each day so many of us have enough life to hold back the inevitable one more moment."

"You sure you're not a preacher?" Celeste chimed in from the back seat. "I didn't know Germans had rhythm like that." She held her phone up to her ear to take another call.

"This is a massive preamble to my question," I nudged sarcastically.

"Hey, we produced Beethoven," Gerda rejoined.

Celeste leaned her head up toward Gerda and said, with a laugh, "Beethoven who?"

I saw an opening for a dad joke and I took it. "You've heard that a few weeks after Beethoven was buried, they could hear his music coming from his grave, right? Except all his music was backward."

"Really?" Gerda asked with skepticism.

"Yeah," I replied. "He was decomposing."

"Oh, God help us," Celeste said.

I wondered about Gerda's hypothesis about the afterlife. Had I missed it? "I don't remember it amid all the other atheistic proselytizing you're trying to sell me," I said.

Gerda laughed and replied, "Yes. I suppose I am trying to convert you to the Dark Side."

"Okay, then. That's out of the way. You haven't converted me yet."

"So to get back to your question about why I'm choosing green burial," Gerda said, "I feel like embalming is some superficial way Americans make themselves feel like they're better than dirt. It's like they're telling the earth that they're somehow superior and will do their damnedest to deny her their bodies."

It's true. Buried beneath a typical ten-acre American cemetery is enough wood to build forty houses. There are twenty thousand tons of concrete from the vaults, more than nine hundred tons of casket steel, and enough embalming fluid to fill a small swimming pool.

The idea of natural burial accepts the inevitable: that despite concrete, wood, steel, preservative agents, and the idealized attempt at physical immortality, the body will eventually decompose back to dust.

—

We arrived to find Ed standing outside the Green Meadow subsection of Fountain Hill Cemetery. With his bright red fleece underneath a solid brown jacket, he looked like a white-haired Paul Bunyan who had a change of heart and laid down his axe to become a tree hugger. Something about him seemed young. His step was quick and his eyes were focused and fixed, gathering all the information his senses could give him.

I say he seemed young because Green Meadow truly appeared to have inspired him so much as to open up his fountain of youth. He explained that twelve years ago, the Fountain Hill Cemetery, founded in 1872, had exhausted its perpetual care funding. Like many cemeteries that have been affected by the shift away from full burial, Fountain Hill was facing the irony of becoming like all its occupants.

Cemeteries all over the United States are dead, and many, many more are dying. Despite its name, the "perpetual care" that so many cemeteries promise only lasts as long as the money that funds it. And whether it be the rise of cremation and the scattering of cremated remains in forests and on beaches, or the dying of churches and their adjoining cemeteries, the funding to keep the grass cut, the driveways plowed in the winter, and the sexton paid are simply running dry. Sometimes good-hearted locals and the concerned families of the deceased will take it upon themselves to cut the grass and care for the gravestones. But those families and the invested locals only seem to last a generation or two before there's no one left alive to tend to the cemetery.

In other words, almost all cemeteries themselves will eventually die. The ground will one day be repurposed for something else once the cemetery's existence is extinguished from public records. When we embalm and bury in a vault and casket, we aren't really beating nature. We're delaying the inevitable by spoiling our bodies with preservation chemicals that keep the body intact until it's withered and lacks any of the physical nourishment it could have given back to the earth. Although it doesn't have the same ecological footprint, cremation robs the earth of her nutrients just the same.

The millions of concrete vaults we've placed in the land, the millions of steel caskets we've placed in those concrete vaults, and the millions of embalmed bodies we've placed in the steel caskets that are contained in the concrete vault, well, it's a bit overwhelming when you add it all up. And it all communicates that we're rupophobic, which means "fearful of dirt." (I literally learned this word thirty seconds ago when I googled "fearful of dirt.") But I think it's a little more than being afraid of dirt. It's deeper. It's not just that we're afraid of dirt. It's that we're afraid we *are* dirt. We are afraid of becoming the land. Because we're afraid of what that might mean.

Maybe we don't like the idea that the difference between land and us isn't that great. And I think this is what Gerda was getting at. Maybe we're afraid that "dust to dust" is an indictment of our value and worth as human beings. Burial means that we're not special, we're not exceptional, and we aren't limitless. We are ultimately land, earth, and dirt.

Our reaction to this truth is very telling. It's telling because it unmasks our underlying assumption that land is cheap or even worthless. And that's our problem, friend: we've devalued the earth because we think we transcend it. We are it. Our lives are it. This is the problem for nearly every industrialized country on this planet. By thinking we're more than earth, we've been brazen enough to pollute it and destroy it.

Up until Sigmund Freud, many intellectuals focused on what separates humans from animals and creation—and, subsequently, what connects us to God and heaven. We did everything in our intellectual power to transcend the earth and prove we were more than the earth. Freud, however, thought the starting point for understanding human psychology wasn't in transcending our nature but in understanding our most basic, earthbound traits: the sex drive and the death drive.

One of the reasons we've placed so much importance on the human soul is because it's the unseen part of us that we thought was more than dirt. The soul—and not the body— was what connected us to God. Much of Western philosophy and theology is a thorough attempt to disembody us from our flesh. Before the Enlightenment, the idea of the soul was what made humans unlike the animals. Our souls were eternal—or if not eternal, at least immaterial. The soul was that invisible part of us that gave us the ability to connect with God. It was the soul that would live on, after the body had died, into the afterlife.

We've tried so hard to disembody ourselves that we've become strangers to our bodies and fearful of flesh. And we are absolutely terrified of dead flesh.

But Gerda wasn't. She wasn't afraid to die. And she wasn't afraid to allow her body to lose its identity and become dirt. For her, the land was divine, and she was gaining her identity by becoming one with it.

Ed welcomed us to Green Meadow and showed us around. He told us about the rules of the green cemetery, including no embalmed bodies and no permanent headstones. Everything that's buried has to be biodegradable, he said, so ideally caskets buried there are made out of wicker and clothing is made out of linen.

Gerda then explained to Ed that she was dying of cancer and that she was looking forward to giving her ailing body back to the dirt.

"In some ways," she said to Ed, "this place will be my heaven. It will be the place I go when I die." She looked across the field that was Green Meadow and said, "In fact, I think I'd rather go here when I die than go to heaven."

Ed cocked his head to the side, befuddled as to whether he should just ignore Gerda's diss of heaven or say something. His face was expressionless. Gerda read the room and answered the question she assumed Ed's face was asking. "Yes," she said, "I don't believe in an eternal soul. This place is where my afterlife will be."

"Aren't you afraid to die?" Ed asked innocently.

"Not at all," Gerda replied. "Death has been my constant companion through life, motivating me to be better, helping me understand empathy, love, and presence.

"And the land itself is divine, if you stop to think about it," Gerda went on. "It provides us with food, and it gives us shelter. It fathers us and mothers us. And it's been doing this for millions of years," she added. "It sacrifices for us. It dies for us. It lives for us. It calls us to come together. It gives us grace, and it gives us empowerment. We simply wouldn't exist without it. In many ways, the land shares many similar characteristics to the God you worship."

No one said anything, and so Gerda went on. "Why shouldn't I believe it's divine? Why can't I believe that my body's burial in it is similar to heaven?"

—

Land is our soul. Land is our life. Land is our worth. Land is us. We need to turn our assumption that land is worthless on its head by affirming the value of it all. When I hear that I should give my body back to the land, it should make me grateful to become a part of something so magical, mysterious, and wonderful. Giving our bodies to the land isn't an indictment of our declining value; it's a proclamation of our worth.

It's important to remember that green burial isn't new. It was practiced in this land long before Europeans landed here. Indeed, while it's good to allow nature to follow its natural course with green burial, we're not inventing something new here. Europeans didn't just come to America and destroy the bodies of the numerous Indigenous nations and take their lands; we also destroyed their dead bodies. Many of us of European descent have trouble understanding how dead bodies are connected to living bodies, and how disrespecting one means we disrespect both.

Western culture has been soulless, in fact, when it comes to death and ancestors. I understand the value of scientific research, but too often it's been a guise for colonization, especially when white people have taken the dead from Indigenous graves to put in our museums and universities in the name of "research" and "education." Hundreds of thousands of Indigenous graves have been dug up. There's still an estimated one hundred and ten thousand Native remains in institutions and museums, and hundreds of thousands of funeral artifacts of Native people.

I'd seen Native cultural artifacts in museums, and it had never occurred to me that many are likely from graves. For most of my life, I'd never thought how disrespectful the whole thing is. Those bodies and their graves are a part of their community, part of their land, and part of the meaning of their people. If white people knew the value of ancestors and the meaning of dead bodies and their oneness with the land, maybe we wouldn't have ripped the soul from the land. "It's just a dead body" is the prevailing attitude today. But individualism on the part of white people has blinded us.

White people finally understand it's wrong to own an individual, but we still can't understand why it's wrong to own ancestors and why taking the dead from their land is the ultimate act of disrespect. The Native dead aren't just artifacts; they are the souls of their people.

Fast forward three hundred years. Imagine that the United States has been invaded by another people who have pushed the US citizens they've left alive into small villages. Imagine going to a museum and seeing dead, embalmed bodies on display. Imagine if one of those embalmed bodies on display was a part of your community.

When both your ancestors and your life are connected to the land, the land is a part of you. There's a oneness with the land that's hard for many of us to understand because we so frequently buy, sell, flip, and move. I own two acres with my house. So I have monetary investment in the land, and I take care of the land. I've literally bled clearing some thorn bushes, and I sweat every time I weed-whack it. But none of my relatives are buried in my yard, nor do I gather my food and resources from my land. My yard isn't a generational land that Wildes have worked and lived off for multiple generations.

Most of us don't survive off our personal land, and fewer still have burial grounds on their land that house generations of their family members. If you did, there'd be a soul connection to the land. If that land were taken from you, it wouldn't just take away your resources; it would take away your soul.

So it's best to be careful when we talk about green burial as a new idea. Let's be careful when we promote it as some progressive movement that aligns with our ecological sentiments. Do I think it's important? Yes. I'm like Gerda. I want green burial for my own body. But for those of us who descend from settler colonialists, let's remember that the very ground we're being buried in carries the souls of peoples our ancestors dispossessed from it.

—

On the way home, Gerda told us exactly what she wanted when she was buried in Green Meadows. She told us how the land she had lived on and the land she was going to be buried in was the land of the Lenni Lenape people, who lived and stewarded the land for some ten thousand years before immigrants arrived some three hundred and fifty years ago.

"Settlers have been on this land for only .035 percent of time during the last ten thousand years," she said. "It's only right that I acknowledge the original stewards when I get buried in it." She wanted a land acknowledgment read at her graveside service as a tribute to the Lenni Lenape inhabitants. She read us the end of that land acknowledgment on the way back to Parkesburg: "In our acknowledgment of the continued presence of Lenape people in their homeland, we affirm the aspiration of the great Lenape Chief Tamanend, that there be harmony between the indigenous people of this land and the descendants of the immigrants to this land, 'as long as the rivers and creeks flow, and the sun, moon, and stars shine.'"

"I don't know how the Lenape people want harmony with us after all we've done to them," Gerda said. "But if that's what they want, giving my body to this land—at this stage in my life—may be the most harmonious thing I can do."

CHAPTER 11

OMINOUS FORECAST

Long days were becoming commonplace at the funeral home. But on the eve of the global pandemic, the whole term "long day" was just a few weeks shy of being redefined.

The feeling in late February and early March 2020 was not unlike the sense of impending doom we feel on the East Coast as news stations report on the imminent arrival of a hurricane. Leading up to landfall, there's a heaviness in the air. A pensive waiting. In the days before the hurricane, the skies are usually clear, and if you didn't know what was coming, they would seem like just any other day. But the sky eventually darkens, the winds pick up, and you sit inside, waiting, helpless and at the mercy of the storm's wrath.

As the pandemic made landfall in the late winter of 2020, it became pretty obvious that, in addition to hospitals and medical clinics, the deathcare industry was going to take a direct hit. We had already seen what the pandemic was doing to Bergamo, Italy, where funeral homes were dealing with five to six times their normal amount of work. Funeral directors were running out of room for the bodies, and funerals weren't even a possibility.

There were so many deaths that the obituary section of the Bergamo newspaper had nine to ten pages compared to their normal one or two. In Spain, the body count was so overwhelming that they used an ice rink to keep the deceased from decomposing.

So I began scrambling to prepare for the potential of Bergamo. My sense of foreboding grew more ominous when, one afternoon in late February 2020, about six months after traveling to Green Meadow Cemetery, I dusted off our old ledger book from the early 1900s. At that time, we were a small funeral home that could only support one full-timer—my great-great-grandfather, William Wilde—and one part-timer—William's twenty-five-year-old son, James W. Wilde, my great-grandfather. I paged through the ledger book carefully, trying not to snap the deteriorating paper that had survived more than 120 years.

The lines of the ledger were filled with itemized funeral costs, delineated under the name of the deceased—such as one Edward Moore, who died on November 27, 1918. Moore happened to have the most expensive funeral of the year:

$150.00 for square oak casket

$12.00 for pine case

$8.00 for embalming body

$18.00 for suit of clothes

$4.90 for under clothes, shirt, and stockings

$1.00 for shaving

$0.75 for newspaper notice to *Local + Record*

$4.00 for name plate

$10.00 for service and attendance of funeral

$10.00 for expenses to Lancaster

$7.00 for opening and closing grave

$6.50 for blanket and handkerchief

$232.15 = Total

From 1899—the first year of the ledger book—to 1917, the funeral home averaged forty death cases per year. Then the 1918 influenza pandemic hit. The funeral home handled one hundred cases in 1918 alone. I wish I had the old ledger books for the Brown Funeral Home, my mother's family business, because it would have been interesting to see how their caseload increased during the pandemic. Even though I don't have those numbers, I'm sure it was a stressful time for my maternal forbearers as well.

As I closed the ledger book, I closed my eyes and took a deep breath. In 2019, before the pandemic hit, we had had nearly 300 death cases—a load that nearly maxed us out. If the pandemic doubled our death cases like the 1918 pandemic had ... well, we'd have to play Tetris with dead bodies to fit them throughout the funeral home.

To avoid such a game of Tetris—even a neat and respectful one—I knew I needed to find alternate ways to store dead bodies. While many residents of the Commonwealth of Pennsylvania were stocking up on hand sanitizer, toilet paper, and, apparently, ammo, I was on the phone trying to order a new removal cot and a cooler. "Cooler" is funeral industry speak for a refrigerator designed to store dead bodies. We had two coolers, which held a total of four bodies combined, and I knew that wasn't going to be enough when COVID-19 made its way to Parkesburg.

I ended up buying a cooler from a funeral supply business run by a friend of mine, T. R. Ward, who told me he'd give me some perks if I shared the purchase and let him advertise his business on my *Confessions of a Funeral Director* Facebook page. I'm sure I made the social media influencer gods proud of me when I shared my cooler purchase on the web. Who else can claim that their sponsored post got them free shipping on a dead body storage unit?

Social media also helped me hire extra help. When Angie followed me on Instagram a few years back, I noticed she was in the Northampton Funeral Service program, the same program I had graduated from back in the early 2000s. Angie had graduated a year or so earlier, and—as is often the case for aspiring funeral directors who weren't born into the business like I was—she was having trouble finding a job. She messaged me that she wanted to meet and discuss ways that she could get her foot in the door of the funeral home business. In a not-so-uncommon experience among millennials trying to land a job at a funeral home, she wondered if her tattoos were off-putting to the funeral homes that had already interviewed her. After looking at her résumé and scrolling through her Instagram and seeing what she was about, I decided to see if she'd want to give our funeral home a shot. Angie ended up being a godsend during the pandemic. Her work ethic and positivity—especially in the face of the absolutely maddening task of wrangling doctors to get death certificates signed—helped us stay sane.

Like everyone else in the funeral industry, we struggled to find adequate PPE, personal protective equipment. Our glove supply was low, and we were having trouble finding a supplier. We had face masks, but only a few of the N95 variety that supposedly could protect us from COVID.

Beyond the issue of extra space for dead bodies and enough supplies, however, there was also capacity-building on a personal level. The complications that accompanied the coronavirus—social, political, and emotional—would prove to be almost more than many of us could bear. This was especially true for those of us with a front-row seat to the death-dealing havoc the pandemic was wreaking.

—

Deathcare workers aren't afraid of many conversation topics. You want to talk about bodily fluids and anatomy? Deathcare workers have seen it all. You want to talk about weird sex stuff? Deathcare workers probably know someone who died while doing it. You want to talk about the weirdness of humanity? Deathcare workers have some stories to tell. And God? We have some thoughts, and we're probably okay with yours.

We don't flinch at difficult conversations. In a culture that avoids difficult conversations, funeral directors can actually be refreshing. But here's the thing: our mental health likely suffers because of all the difficult stuff we're conversant in. Difficult conversation topics have a way of accruing in this business, and a job made up of one hard thing piled on top of another on top of another on top of another—well, it can be exhausting.

A few months before the pandemic, I had been struggling to swim in the ocean of depression. The topic of depression is equally a party pleaser as the topic of death. But since I'm comfortable talking and thinking about death, I'm also comfortable talking and thinking about depression.

Like many people found, the pandemic stripped away the parts of our job that made it meaningful. The difficulty of deathcare is eased by the ways we can provide value and service to the bereaved people who come through the funeral home's front doors. The "I'm in this to serve people" answer—which most deathcare workers give to the inevitable "Why do you do this work?"—is as common a line as it is true. A sense of service to our community sustains us. But during the pandemic, the combination of quarantine and an overwhelming workload threatened to take that away.

The pandemic would also threaten to turn our funeral home into a dead person factory. At times, we were so overwhelmed with dead bodies that it robbed us of all the deeply personal interactions that inspire us to stay in deathcare. Without those connections, and with an increased workload that meant dealing with even more death than usual, I was worried for myself. Becoming a worker in a funeral factory held no appeal.

In the beginning of the pandemic, there seemed to be solid evidence that COVID-19 was not going to be as deadly for children as it was for adults. I deeply hoped that was true, because I didn't think I could have done what my great-great-grandfathers and great-grandfathers Wilde and Brown did during the last pandemic. During the influenza of 1918—the year that nearly tripled our funeral home's workload—twenty-three out of their one hundred death calls were children. Can you imagine if children's lives were put at risk by the virus like they were in the 1918 pandemic? As the father of two young children, I couldn't stomach the idea of burying even more children than we already did as part of our work.

Beyond the emotional burden of our increased work-load was the skepticism about mask wearing by people who doubted the dangers of COVID-19. In our area, there was a lot of skepticism and distrust of public health officials. In the beginning of the pandemic, many of our *Fox News* devotees thought the coronavirus was no more dangerous than the flu. Numerous conspiracy theories were floating around—like the one in which doctors were supposedly only includ-ing the coronavirus on death certificates to get a monetary kickback. I heard some variety of this joke on multiple occa-sions: "If you get killed in a motorcycle accident, you know what the death certificate will say? COVID-19."

Whenever someone would suggest to me that the number of virus-related deaths were exaggerated, I'd shoot back by telling them that every single family that we served whose loved one died from the virus were convinced that the death was indeed from COVID. Even families who were not con-vinced by mainstream understandings of the virus *became* convinced by the disturbing symptoms—symptoms that so quickly turned fatal it was like nothing the family had seen before.

People can lie about a lot of things in life, like their age or how much money they make. People can even lie to themselves about who they are or who they are not. But death? It's the purest truth. It's the great reality that cuts through all the lies, because you can't fake life. You can pump a dead body full of embalming fluid, dress it up, and get the makeup just right, but that body is still ... dead. Because you can't fake life no matter how hard you try.

When people look at this unadulterated truth of death—as so many families were forced to do during the pandemic—it can do one of two things. The reality of death can go deep into every part of a person's being, molding them into honest humans who are able to accept their vulnerabilities, inadequacies, and limitations. Death can motivate people to accept their circumstances and to use the remainder of their time to fully live.

Or a person can take a less painful but much more tedious path of denial. This is why a dishonest funeral director is such an ugly thing. It's not because they're just lying about costs and trying to upsell their products; ugly people in every industry lie about costs and try to upsell. What makes dishonest funeral directors *extra* ugly is that they've had a front-row seat to pure truth ... and they've chosen to work incredibly hard to suppress it.

When a life has been spent denying vulnerability and limitations—in a space like a funeral home that's supposed to embrace mortality—well, it twists and turns a soul into something so inhuman that there's nothing real left. I personally know a few of these funeral directors.

As best as I can, I've tried to choose acceptance. I've tried to avoid denial and to be as honest and transparent and accepting of death as I can be. Denial seemed to win the day in many parts of the country in response to the coronavirus, and that was frustrating beyond words.

Then again, acceptance has its own consequences.

—

Sometimes, in the middle of a pandemic workday, I'd ask myself the question, What if the coronavirus were killing children at the rate that the pandemic of 1918 did? Would antimask sentiments have been as strong if a higher percentage of coronavirus deaths had been children? I don't think we need to imagine the lengths parents would have taken to protect their children. I don't think we would have heard the complaints about mask wearing and social distancing. I don't think we would have been as tolerant of conspiracy theories. In fact, if we look back at polio and its disproportionate effects on children, we see that fewer adults had the same antagonism toward the vaccine.

But the coronavirus adversely affected older adults and the immunocompromised, and apparently our society just wasn't much interested in protecting them. Because, as someone said to me at a funeral during the pandemic, older adults "are probably going to die anyway." Or here's another line that I heard on a number of occasions: "COVID is just thinning the herd."

This attitude is significant because it speaks to our society's ageism. We would have been willing to go to any measure to protect our children, but to protect our aged and sick? Losing children is probably the most difficult experience in human existence, as it ends a story way too soon. When we lose our older adults, however, we lose the other end of that. We lose a story that's nearing its completion. Much like a book, theirs is a story that can provide stability, or a cautionary tale, or a love that's been matured by time and work, or wisdom found only when the parts of the story come together in a conclusion. In the death of children, a story is cut short before it can be written. But when we lose our older people, it's like we're losing the book.

There's also an attitude that sees work and results as defining a person's worth. "What do you do for a living?" is the question you usually get asked by a stranger at a party or a social event. That rubric for judging a person's importance implies that if you aren't producing, you must be a burden to society. Many older people who have grown up feeling that their value is in their work are not necessarily afraid of dying; they're afraid of "becoming a burden."

Visual ageism doesn't help in our attitude toward older people. We see few older heroes represented in the media. Heroism is a young person's game, or at least that's what we see. But what of the hero grandparent who steps in to help their daughter with a newborn child and no partner and no income? I don't know how many grandmothers and grandfathers I've buried who were like second parents to their grandchildren, helping support them and raise them to be whole, well-rounded children. When grandchildren are frequently in the presence of grandparents, those grandchildren reap a real inheritance: knowing how to live life.

Wisdom is the voice of the ancestors. It leads the way through dark valleys. It calls to us when we're lost. It gives us strength to take the next step. Wisdom is the trail sign and road marker left by those who went before us. These signs help guide us, and if we listen, wisdom takes us further than we could have ever gone on our own. Wisdom is part of the afterlife. It's a way the dead still speak. When our older people perceive their value to lie only in their ability to work rather than in their wisdom, we all suffer.

With globalization and the accessibility of the internet, people have rapidly evolved in their understanding of the world. A ninety-year-old person's understanding of the world is going to be drastically different from a twenty-year-old's because of the exposure social media gives us. But understanding the world isn't the definition of wisdom or value. Perhaps we've valued knowledge over wisdom. Perhaps we've valued exposure over experience, and technological interface above the elderly authority.

Many of us have a linear view of time, where the past is somehow dead, the future is what's coming, and the present is all we have. While that perspective is certainly true when we're defining time by a clock, it's not the way time works with people. Time is a confluence of past, present, and future. If we really want to understand ourselves in real time, we have to understand our ancestors. All the progress that we see, all the massive advances that we're witnessing right now, these are theirs just as much as they're ours. It's just that we're reaping the reward, with the hope that what we do today affects our children's future.

We can often tell how much we love ourselves by how we love our older people. If the "coronavirus is thinning the herd" perspective has taught me anything, it's that those who disregard our older people also disregard our past, our present, and our future.

I know that was a rant, but it's one that loops all the way back to attitudes I confronted during the pandemic. For the most part, people were understanding, especially around funerals. As the pandemic wore on, even people who were ardently against mask wearing would wear them to funerals. But the process of getting those people to that point was laborious, and everything required to get us there felt heavy.

If society were more collectivist, and if we had higher regard for older people and those at risk—well, then we could have spent our energies during an exhausting worldwide pandemic on other things.

—

All the way up to the start of the pandemic, Pop-Pop refused to stop working at the funeral home, despite what his body was telling him. He'd wander over nearly every day to see what was going on and to give solicited or unsolicited commentary on how we were running the funeral home. It gave him something to do and a routine that kept his body moving.

I loved the fact that he wanted to keep working. Many of us work jobs that grind so hard against our souls that we look forward to retirement age so we can pursue things we want to do instead of things we have to do.

But Pop-Pop never had any intention of retiring. In fact, when my dad retires in a few years, he will be the first Wilde to actually *retire* from the funeral business. Every generation of Wilde funeral directors have stayed in the business until their health kept them from it. For Pop-Pop—and, I imagine, for his father before him, and his father before that—working in the funeral industry at a later age is when you really start taking care of your own generation. You bury longtime friends, schoolmates, and contemporaries. There is, I suppose, the feeling of fulfilling a solemn duty in laying your peers to rest.

"I just don't have any pep today, Calebee," Pop-Pop would tell me as he came in for work in the morning. The other line that he'd often use was, "I'm thirty years old from my neck on up, but the rest of me is old."

His declining physical capacity was difficult for him to accept. He had been the lead funeral director at our funeral home for most of his career, due to both his personality and his work ethic. Even into his late eighties, he still had the same personality and the same ethic. But he no longer had the "pep" to make funeral arrangements, work funerals, or embalm bodies. After those three tasks, the rest of this job is punching keyboards, making removals, and answering the incessant call of the business phone. Pop-Pop could never really "work the computer," as he said, and he had stopped making removals in his early seventies. Then, because he was increasingly out of the loop, he didn't feel like he could answer the phone and the real-time funeral questions from those who were calling.

But the love from the Parkesburg community only increased as he aged out of the day-to-day workings of the business. Almost every family I met with would ask, "How's

Bud?" And if Pop-Pop did happen to have the pep to show up for a funeral on any given day, he immediately became an emblem of comfort. Everyone would meander over to where he had decided to sit down, give him hugs and kisses, and strike up a conversation either about his health or about times gone by. It felt like he was living history in flesh, able to recount names, events, and stories from a bygone era. Pop-Pop seemed like a living embodiment of a bygone Parkesburg generation, and when people saw him, it was like they were seeing their own parents or grandparents.

Having known so many and buried so many of Parkesburg's dead, Pop-Pop was like the ancestral heart of the community. All of this work at the funeral home, from his teens to his late eighties, garnered him an award ceremony in February 2020, right before the pandemic hit. Pop-Pop was given the highest honor from Lions Club International for extraordinary community service. A Pennsylvania senator, along with some local politicians and a number of community leaders, attended the award presentation. The mayor presented a proclamation from the Borough of Parkesburg that named Pop-Pop's birthday, March 2, "Bud Wilde Day."

Pop-Pop was eighty-eight when the pandemic started, and when it did, he stopped coming to the funeral home entirely. When he stopped coming to the funeral home, it not only took away his motivation for movement, it hurt his identity. He was almost entirely out of the loop at the funeral home, and when he did hear about some of the decisions I was making in terms of handling business during the pandemic, he didn't like it. I had to tell myself that it wasn't necessarily *me* he disapproved of but the fact that he no longer had his hands in the workings of the business. As the pandemic wore on and he became less and less active, his physical strength started to decrease even more. But something else happened in Pop-Pop's demeanor that gave me clarity in my own life.

While Pop-Pop wasn't doing what he loved anymore, his ability to love his family seemed to actually increase—and his love for my dad, specifically. Being away from the funeral home removed the business layer of their relationship. Over the years, as Dad had grown in his capabilities as a funeral director and Pop-Pop had aged, there had been a tension in management styles. But as Pop-Pop lost his control over the day-to-day operations of the funeral home and his physical abilities failed, Dad picked up some of the responsibilities Pop-Pop could no longer carry. As this happened, a stress was lifted from Pop-Pop—a stress that he may have never known he carried. I'd like to think the pandemic actually made Pop-Pop into a better man, one able to sink his love and generosity into his family.

I've never known my dad or Pop-Pop away from the funeral home. I'd get glimpses of my dad when we were on vacation as children. But this was the first I'd ever seen Pop-Pop away from the funeral home. It had been so much of his identity that I'm not sure he knew who he was.

On the eve of my forties, I don't know what my adult self looks like away from the funeral home. Watching Pop-Pop, I began to wonder, What am I like away from the stress and heaviness of death and funerals? Who am I apart from this business of dying?

Unlike Pop-Pop, I want to meet that man. I want to give him more than nine months to live.

CHAPTER 12

CONJURE TOGETHER, RIGHT NOW

The day after the Centers for Disease Control and Prevention (CDC) announced that gatherings of fifty people or more were prohibited, the funeral home was notified of the death of a forty-seven-year-old woman named Diane.

After talking with Diane's daughter, I scheduled the family to come into the funeral home the following day at two in the afternoon to make funeral arrangements. On cue the next day, Diane's husband, mother, and two high school–aged daughters were standing at our funeral home's porch, waiting for me to open the door.

Her family was exhausted. I could see it in their faces. As I would come to find out, Diane's brain aneurysm was unexpected and sudden. She was standing in the doorway of her home, told her husband she felt strange, and immediately collapsed. The EMTs kept her alive, and for a few days the family sat vigilantly by her hospital bed, waiting to find out if this was her end or the beginning of a long recovery process. After many tests they received their answer, and they were by her side when the ventilator was removed.

Diane's funeral arrangements were the first I would make since the CDC's recommendation, and I wasn't exactly sure what to do. How was I going to honor that recommendation when many people in my area still believed the coronavirus to be no worse than the flu?

I opened the funeral home's door and ushered Diane's family into our conference area. After we had spent a half hour together and I had listened to the family tell Diane's story, I felt like I had gained enough trust to talk about the CDC's recommendation. I paused, took a deep breath, and said, "I know you all have been in the hospital for the last couple of days and that you may not have been following the news. But the coronavirus has become a legitimate public health threat. The CDC suggests no public gatherings over fifty people."

They all looked at me, trying to decide if I was really brazen enough to follow through with my line of thinking. I was. I continued. "I'm recommending that you have a private service for only your family and intimate friends."

Their faces displayed a combination of anger and assertiveness, grief and hopelessness. As I had learned from the stories they had just told me, Diane had a large network. She served in the ladies' auxiliary for two local fire companies, she was very involved in her church, and she helped manage all of her daughters' sports teams.

"Diane deserves a big sendoff," her husband responded instinctually. "I need everyone who loved Diane to come together for a funeral."

I had assumed that would be their response, and I was prepared to help them have the funeral they wanted. We scheduled it for the following Thursday at Diane's church. They expected a few hundred people to attend the service.

Two days before Diane's funeral was to take place, her husband called. "I don't want to do this," he said. "In fact, it's the last thing I want to do. But I'm going to make this funeral private."

I wondered whether he heard the surprise in my silence on the other end of the line. "I just can't put the people who loved her at risk," he continued. "We're going to cancel the public service. I don't want her friends and family to have to choose between honoring Diane and putting their health at risk."

I listened to him and tried to affirm his decision. I have to admit that it was hard to hear him grieve over lost grief. But it was a foretaste of things to come. We wouldn't just be witnessing an overwhelming amount of tragic deaths; we'd be witnessing people grieving the loss of communal grieving.

—

I had told my family that if the coronavirus drastically increased our workload at the funeral home, I would just move into the funeral home. At that point, we didn't really know if people could contract the coronavirus from dead bodies, and we knew we'd still have to work with families in some capacity. There was pretty good evidence that the virus was not a great risk to children, but I didn't want to carry the virus home to my kids and my wife if I could help it.

A month before the pandemic kicked into gear in the United States, Nathan—the first non-Wilde funeral director at the funeral home—and I had decided we could crash at the funeral home together if things got bad. He was young and living at home with his parents, and he didn't want to put his parents at risk. The funeral home's attic has a room that my aunt and uncle had lived in right after Mom-Mom Wilde passed away in 1992. They lived there to keep Pop-Pop company as he adjusted to Mom-Mom's death. And while the room had accumulated a lot of junk between 1992 and 2020, it was still livable.

So as the pandemic intensified in March 2020, Nathan and I moved all the old furniture and discarded electronics from the 1990s out of the attic space, and we cleaned it from floor to ceiling to prepare for the good possibility that we'd be its new temporary residents. I bought two cots for us to sleep on, and we waited to see if the pandemic was going to be as bad as we thought.

On April 10, the day after we had three COVID death calls in one day, Nathan and I moved into the attic. We ended up staying through the first surge, which lasted a little over a month.

That first month was physically exhausting, as we were working late into the night and sometimes right through the night and into the morning. It was a nonstop chaotic ride that felt like we were just holding on to whatever we could to help us survive. The physical exhaustion was just part of the stress we were all carrying. Funeral directors were just trying to figure out what we were supposed to do. Like the rest of the world, we kept getting mixed messages from those around us and those in positions of power above us.

The other part of the exhaustion came from wrestling with questions like, What happens if someone comes to a small, private funeral (the only kind we were allowing) without a mask? Should we turn away antimaskers (of which there were many) from a funeral? And if we don't turn them away if they refuse to wear a mask, and if they happen to spread virus at the event, will the funeral home be liable to lawsuits?

Should we wipe down the register book pen every time a funeral-goer signs their name?

Should we rope the family off from the public visitation line so they aren't hugged by every well-wishing attender?

Should we even have funerals at all?

In retrospect, it's easy to look at those questions with the knowledge that we have now, but in real time, these questions nagged at my mind. We just tried our best. Like so many people everywhere, we did the best we could.

And then there were the specific questions surrounding the handling of bodies during this time. Can we get COVID from a dead body? What should we do if we have a death call for someone who died at home from the coronavirus? Should we even go since the houseful of mourners has been exposed? And if we do go and we are exposed, then what?

Those were the questions in my mind when I talked to a Sadsbury Township police officer at two in the morning. When I arrived at the deceased's house, the officer was standing in the parking lot, waiting to greet me. I got out of the removal van and walked over to her. Right away, she let me know that the deceased had been diagnosed with COVID only a few days prior.

"Isn't the coroner going to take the body?" I asked the offi-cer. At this point in the pandemic, all the COVID remov-als I had made either came from a hospital or a quarantined section of a nursing home. This was my first COVID home removal. But as the pandemic grew in the coming months, it wouldn't be my last.

She replied in a pragmatic and assertive voice, "The coro-ner just told me over the phone that they're overwhelmed. They need you to make the removal."

"The deceased tested positive for the virus a few days ago," she told me. "He went to bed earlier than his wife, and when she came to crawl into bed with him, he was dead. He was only sixty-five years old."

"Did he have any preexisting conditions?" I asked.

"Not that the family knows of. When I got here, I gave him CPR, but it was too late. He was already cold at that point."

"Wait." I paused. "You gave him CPR? Um, what's the pro-tocol for your department? Aren't you required to quaran-tine after you do CPR on someone who tested positive?"

Her body straightened. It was like her posture had been weighed down by all the little things that were adding up during the pandemic. Like so many of us during the pan-demic, she tried to find her confidence.

"I can't," she responded, with a face that made it seem like I was asking a rhetorical question. "Our department doesn't have enough officers as it is. We're just like the coroner's office: stretched to the max. I'll only quarantine if I develop symptoms."

Many first responders were faced with such questions—questions with no good answer, and ones that posed ethical dilemmas. Hospice workers and hospice chaplains like Celeste were no different. Most hospice nurses, like funeral directors, were guided by contextual decision-making that depended on the situation they found themselves in. Everyone has stories about struggles during COVID, whether it was financial, marital, existential, or health. Unless you were Jeff Bezos, you lost something.

Yet the ethical struggles many of us faced carried their own kind of stress. Like I said before, we all just did the best we knew how with the resources we had. That was all we could do.

We ended up having fifty COVID cases in 2020, pushing our caseload to three hundred and fifty for the year, fifty cases more than we had the year before. It was a far cry from the threefold increase that our funeral home had experienced in 1918, but it was still enough to make us tired. It was tiring for so many reasons. Tiring because we didn't always know the right way to approach the pandemic. Tiring because everyone in our area seemed to have a different opinion about what safety measures should and should not be taken. And tiring to see so many grieving families disheartened by having their outlet for communal grief taken away.

There's an old adage you may have heard that goes something like this. A person dies two times: one time when they stop breathing, and a second time when somebody says their name for the last time.

Our culture allows the second death to start shortly after the first one. With the frequent call for "closure," the desire for a neat and tidy grief process, and the general denial of death, we fear the first one. And thus we hasten the second.

In a culture still under the sway of Enlightenment notions, we are asked to bury our dead twice: once in the ground, and then again in our hearts. I think Diane's husband originally felt like that's what I was asking him to do by suggesting the private service: bury his wife's memory quickly and prevent her friends and loved ones from keeping her alive with them as long as possible.

—

Not every culture rushes its inhabitants along toward denial and closure. The Aztecs did their best to make sure the second death—the forgetting of those who have passed—didn't happen on their watch. For one whole month after the harvest, the Aztecs would honor and celebrate their ancestors by visiting their tombs, which were sometimes under their houses so the dead could stay close. During this time they would prepare meals and invite the spirits of their dead to come and dwell with the living. Like those in many other cultures, they believed that the end of the harvest created a place where the boundaries that stand between the living and the dead become transparent.

When the Spanish invaded in the sixteenth century, the colonizers attempted to stomp out and replace the Aztec traditions with Catholicism's All Saints Day and All Souls Day. The remnant of the Aztec tradition thus morphed into the celebration of Día de Los Muertos. In the spirit of the old tradition, the skull sugar candies, skeletons, and caskets are all meant to be an irreverent confrontation with death that underscore the main message of the tradition: We won't let the second death take our family. This isn't just a "Mexican Halloween," as some have represented it. Día de Los Muertos makes a mockery of the second death by celebrating the deceased.

Día de Los Muertos invites the children of the Aztecs to embrace the thin space between death and life, to lean into it, to raise their fists to the second death, and to celebrate their dead. We sometimes think that celebration and death are categorical opposites—that one can't dwell with the other. We fear that bringing up our dead solemnizes life. But festivities and death can dwell together. Keeping our dead alive by speaking their names is something to celebrate.

Just as there are two deaths—one when we die, and again when we're forgotten—there are also two births. Funerals, traditionally, begin the second birth. They are the beginning of new life. In a way, a funeral is a birth into the afterlife. Funerals validate the name of the deceased, they bring family together, and they are often religious in nature. And almost like we do with our children, we keep them alive with our love and our effort. Funerals acknowledge that the afterlife resides with us.

So many families who lost loved ones were deprived of a funeral during the pandemic. Given this fact, and given Western culture's general rush toward closure, we may need to give a little more attention to active remembering. So often, our remembering is passive. Memories of the deceased are sparked by a holiday, a smell, or the sound of a sports broadcast.

Active remembering occurs when we take steps to memorialize the deceased. Perhaps it's a small shrine in your bedroom. Perhaps it's a remembrance gathering with family and friends on the anniversary of your loved one's death. For some, it's a garden bed planted along the side of your house with the favorite perennials of your loved one.

Like Gerda's original attitude of avoiding a funeral for Noshi, you'd think that the pandemic might be the catalyst to bring about the death of funerals. Just like the pandemic had us reexamining work spaces, school spaces, and community spaces, it also made us reexamine death spaces. You would think that perhaps the small, private funerals of the pandemic would have sped up this cultural desire to "just burn my ass." You'd think the pandemic would have given us all the opportunity to see how unnecessary funerals really are.

And maybe it will. I'm not a futurist, so I can't make any predictions based on case studies and cultural trends. What I can say is that I saw the opposite sentiment during the pandemic. I saw families not only grieve the loss of their loved ones, I saw them grieve the loss of shared grief. It turns out that the loss of shared grief is a heavier burden to bear than most of us thought. Closure is not the end to grief that so many of us have thought. Having a quick grieving process that either devalues a funeral or throws it out altogether isn't as helpful as we thought. Grief is just the end product of love, and love doesn't always know the difference between what's alive and what's dead. Love just is.

When the person we love dies, that doesn't mean our love just dies too. As my friend Megan Devine writes in her paradigm-shifting book, *It's OK That You're Not OK,* "Some things in life cannot be fixed. They can only be carried." It also turns out that what we carry can be lighter when we can share it with others.

—

A few years ago, I had a vision. To explain the vision, I'm going to ask that you step into the shoes of the person telling the story. Imagine with me that this is something you're experiencing in real time.

Some might call this vision a conjuring. In the Christian church, we might call it communion. Others still might call it a funeral of the imagination. Whatever it is, it helped me understand the connections between myself and those who have gone before and is a way to avoid letting the deceased die twice.

I'm standing in the middle of a field. It is nearing dusk, and the temperature is perfectly comfortable. To my right, there's an open pavilion, with about thirty people holding conversations about a loved one lost. It's a funeral of sorts, set outside.

As I stand in the field, I can hear the chatter of my loved one's friends and family. I close my eyes to remember my times with the deceased, and as I do, my chest starts to get warm. I can feel something pulsing inside, and it isn't beating to the rhythm of my heart.

I open my eyes, and small lights—like marble-sized stars—slowly start emptying out of my chest. Some are radiant, while others are less so. Some are dancing, and others are moving slowly. Still others bob and weave all over, like a leaf in the autumn wind. After a few hundred have left my chest, they start to form a pattern. After a few moments, they find a rhythm that seems to breathe as they gather in and then exhale out.

The breathing goes on for about a minute before I notice everyone has come and gathered in a circle around the stars. As they do, stars are coming out of their chests, and the gathering lights at the center of our circle become as blinding as the sun. We shield our eyes with our hands as the lights get brighter, eventually covering our eyes to keep ourselves from being blinded.

As the lights gather, the air becomes familiar, like the smell of the air in your childhood home or your living room when your family gathers to play a game. The brightness of the lights slowly begins to fade, and I slowly allow my eyes to open. At first, the light is too blinding to make out what is happening. I don't know how long it takes for the light to dim. Time takes a deep breath and calms itself.

A shape starts forming, and as it does, the light becomes less and less bright. Suddenly, bolts of what look like lightning reach out to each of us, landing squarely on each of our chests. Like umbilical cords, the bolts begin pumping life into whatever is growing in our midst.

Soon we see what appears to be feet forming on the ground. Hands come next, then legs, arms, torso, chest, and head. We all stand in silence as we begin to see features form on the face. A smile, communicating love to all of us. All at once, we all know.

We all come in closer, and as we do, everyone reaches out and touches what we all know is our dead loved one. Together, we stay like that for a long time, huddled together within the bounds of a family. Some have thick and bright lightning cords flowing between us and our loved one, while others have small ones that are no less important. There is a sense that if even one of us would leave the circle, a piece of our loved one would leave too. There is a sense that each of us holds a part that makes up the whole.

The darkness falls as the sun sets. We stay huddled together, sustained by the light that we have all created.

—

During my most monk-like days in high school, when I was daily meditating on the Bible and praying both in communal and personal spaces, I felt close to God. You might say that it's all in my head, and I'd say yes. Yes, it is. Because there's a very distinct possibility that our loved ones—God, even— somehow take up space in our minds.

Like we do with the bread and wine during the Eucharist, we have communion and remember. We remember the one who has been scattered across all the hearts they touched during their lifetime. Even though I don't believe it literally, I like the idea of transubstantiation: the notion that when we partake of the Eucharist, the bread and wine actually transform into the literal body and blood of Jesus. Scientifically, we know that can't be true. But even if the bread and wine do not become the actual body and blood of Jesus during the sacrament, it may be that, as a person meditates on Jesus and reads the words of scripture, that person's image of Jesus may be as reflective in their own personal lives as it is in their brains. In other words, it's very possible

that our neural pathways begin to mirror the neural pathways of Christ.

As many have pointed out, we become like the things or
people that we love. That "becoming" may be figurative; but
let's not rule out that it could indeed be literal. When scripture talks about having the mind of Christ, it's very possible
that the thought patterns and goals of Christ imprint in our
brains and become a neurological reflection of Christ's.

Images get distorted over time. And Jesus has surely been
distorted and manipulated and exploited by those in power.
If there is one way to keep Jesus's image somewhat accountable to what's displayed in scripture, it's to do it in community. In community, your idea of Jesus isn't just left to its
own. The same is also true of those we remember. Just like
the vision I shared earlier, we can start to see the whole when
we remember together.

When, for whatever reason, funerals are taken away
from us—when we can't remember with friends and family
and when we have to grieve on our own—we may only be
remembering a small portion of the deceased. That's why
it was so hard on Diane's family and all the other families
who couldn't hold regular funerals during the pandemic:
they knew that their love for Diane was made complete by
the love others had for her. Only together can we all piece
together the whole. The deceased are most alive in our
hearts—especially when those hearts are shared.

Funerals are important for the living, as the adage goes.
But they are also important for the deceased. Funerals—
however they may look, in whatever setting they may take

place—are a key way to keep the dead from experiencing the second death.

It's okay to water the grave. It's okay to talk about your loved one a little more. It's okay to cry longer. It's okay to have a couple of remembrance gatherings as you see fit. If we can remember together, I'm not sure we'll be able to see the whole.

It turns out that the notion of "closure" for our grief isn't just a wrong way of looking at things. It's also a sad idea to believe. We don't have to let our loved ones go; we can take them with us. We can hold their memory proudly and celebrate the fact that as long as we live, we'll forestall the second death.

This isn't a responsibility that we should feel as a burden; it's an avenue for our love. I'm saying that your loved ones are still here. I'm saying that we can still hear them and speak to them. I'm saying that it turns out that we can see them the most clearly when we all gather and conjure them together.

CHAPTER 13

SPEAKING TO GHOSTS

I was on my way back from Glen Run Cemetery, having just finished a graveside service, when I felt my phone buzz in my pocket. My body tightened from anticipation of the orders that could be coming from the other side of the phone. Phone calls at this time of the day are usually my dad or mom letting me know we have a death call. I struggled to get my cell phone out of pants that had become tighter from my pandemic stress-eating sessions. After lifting my butt off the driver's seat to get a straight shot at my phone with my arm, I got my phone and saw it was Gerda.

"Hey, friend," I said, happy to hear her voice on the other end of the phone. "I'm in the hearse," I explained, "and if I lose reception out here in the country, I'll call you back."

"You riding in the front of the hearse or the back?" Gerda asked jokingly.

"I *am* tired, and I thought about lying down in the back," I said, "but I've tried it and it's not comfortable."

Gerda was now under hospice care and currently living at Hickory House Nursing Home. COVID protocols were keeping visitors out, but she was able to do phone calls and FaceTime.

"It's time for me to tell you something. After our trip to Green Meadows, I booked a flight to Germany and flew over to see some of my family."

I could tell that Gerda was just slightly sheepish as she spoke. There was an excitement in her voice when she said she had gone to Germany, but she couldn't yet explain it with the confidence that time and understanding would have given her.

"I tracked my sister down through Facebook. I told her I was dying and that I wanted to come back to Germany and sit down with her and talk," Gerda said.

"I'm guessing she said yes?" I asked.

"I don't know that I gave her much of a choice," Gerda responded. "It's kind of hard to say no to a dying person. I took full advantage of my terminal diagnosis, insisting that I come over as soon as possible because, well, I didn't have too much time left."

Gerda recounted how her sister picked her up at the airport and drove her back to her house, where her other sisters and all their children—Gerda's nieces and nephews—and some other relatives were waiting to meet her. She told us how kind and welcoming her nieces and nephews were to her. They wanted to know about her life, about America, about Noshi. She said they exuded everything she'd ever want in children if she had ever had them. They were smart, open, and just weird enough to make her feel comfortable.

Over the next couple of days, her conversations with her sisters helped fill in the multiple-decade gap from when she left home. Her younger sisters told her that at first they were angry that she had left them at home with their abusive father, but as they became teenagers, they decided that going to university was something they could do because they saw their older sister do it. In the 1950s, it was incredibly difficult for women to get into a university, but her younger sisters knew it was possible from watching Gerda. Like Gerda, they waited until they had graduated and had started their careers before they started a family. They passed that high value on education down onto their children—all because Gerda decided that she was going to make a way for herself by leaving the family.

They told Gerda multiple times that even though they lived in different countries and hadn't spoken in decades, they saw Gerda as the family's matriarch. Her act of rebellion against Hans, by using education as a ladder out of the family, was *the* act that set her sisters and all their families on an entirely different life trajectory.

"After talking to them for a couple of days, I told them that I wanted to visit our parents' gravesites," Gerda said. "I felt empowered, like I had unknowingly beaten their hatred. I often felt like I had just run away from the hatred, but sometimes running away is the change. In the midst of all the abuse of my childhood, all the horrible moments that I've wiped from my mind, I was still able to change the whole trajectory of our family."

She told me what she said at the grave of her parents. It was rather long, so I'm going to paraphrase as best I can remember. As she stood over the grave of her parents and addressed them some fifty years after she had left them, she said something like this:

"Your silence, your bitterness, your belief in inequality, your hatred ... it won't win. I think I've seen the big picture. History is making a path toward love and grace and freedom and equality. You were a massive detour. But you won't win in the future, and you won't win now. Because here, with you, I'm burying my hatred. I'm giving it to you and leaving it here. Love is seeping into every corner of the earth, and now, right here, I'm letting it seep into that dark corner of my heart that you built. I'm tearing down what you built, and I'm changing the future today by bringing the future to the present. You haven't won. You won't win. Your daughter is full of love now. Every corner of her heart is love. The day will come when every corner of the earth will do the same. And on that day, we will grieve every soul that had been infected by hatred.

"I pity you, for all the pain your endured and all the pain you created. You were just repeating the pain that had been passed down to you. I changed it. If your ghosts are still here and you're somehow listening to me, maybe you'll find some consolation in knowing that your pain wasn't passed down to your grandchildren. They're thriving, and their children are thriving. We broke the cycles. In one generation, we broke the cycles. You weren't proud of me when I was young, but I'm proud of what I've become. I'm proud of who I am."

I had been listening with bated breath as Gerda recounted everything. As she neared the end of telling me what she told her parents, Gerda started to cry. We sat there for a holy moment, the kind that feels like all eternity in just a few seconds.

I eventually broke the silence, telling Gerda that I was so happy for her and proud of her and thankful she let me know.

If anything is, I think love is the basis of eternal life. Love is the seed of eternal life, and it's also the dirt, water, and sun that keeps it growing. Eternal life isn't just some static dimension that exists after death. Eternal life is becoming through love. It's becoming with each act of love we extend, with each act of love we receive.

Eternal life is love in process.

—

Every year when Halloween comes around, those classic horror flicks start looping on television, with their dated special effects and well-timed scare scenes that make us jump even though we know they're coming. Who doesn't love seeing children dressed in costumes? The weather. The fall leaves. The pumpkin spice everything. But beneath the cute and fun is a flirtation with the dark side of the spiritual realm, where ghosts, spirits, and hauntings dwell.

In the traditional Irish calendar, there are four "quarter days" each year, one that marks the beginning of each new season. The first of November marked the beginning of winter, considered the "darker half" of the Irish year. But the day *before* the first of November (October 31) was seen as a liminal, in-between period where the otherworld seeped into this world, allowing spirits—some good and others bad—to visit the living.

Instead of shutting their doors and pouring some pre-Christian version of holy water around their houses to keep the spirits away, people in ancient Ireland would often do the exact opposite. They'd open up their homes, set extra places at the dinner table, and even prepare a meal with the hope that maybe the dead would bless them with health and wholeness through the winter months.

I love how the imagination can dance around these ideas. I want to believe in the spiritual kinds of ghosts, but the rational part of my brain usually wins over the mystical. You'd think a funeral director would have seen *something*, right? Maybe a ghost in the prep room where the dead bodies await their disposition. Or something misty and creepy at the cemetery? I am often awake at the witching hours, going on late-night death calls or strolling through the silent corridors of nursing homes. There is a silence to these dark hours, a calm that can be disarming because it's so abnormally restful that it feels empty and alone. But it's never been an eerie silence for me, even when I've been handling the dead. It's true that the tragic deaths—the murders, the suicides, and some grisly accidents—have a presence to them. But I'm not sure if the presence is exactly spiritual or just the weight of the horror.

Maybe I'm wrong. Maybe there are spirits. Maybe the spirits that do exist have always been kind to me because I care for the dead. I'm willing to entertain the maybe.

I do, though, believe in another kind of ghost. One that can be much scarier. Much more damaging. And much more haunting.

There is this liminality between the living and the dead, an in-between where the bonds of love can still dwell. Liminality is something that makes us uncomfortable. We humans like binaries, such as yes or no. On or off. But some things exist in the in-between. They are yes *and* no. Dead *and* alive. Present *and* absent.

The liminality of our dead is like a ghost, like Halloween. Because our loved ones are both gone *and* still here with you. Their actions, character, and—yes, I think I can use this word—*spirit* have literally helped form your neural pathways. The way they thought, the things they said, their little idiosyncrasies—these are all dwelling in you.

Researchers in the field of behavioral epigenetics are finding that our experiences can be passed down on a molecular level. I wrote in my first book, *Confessions of a Funeral Director*, that "there are literal pieces of your loved ones in you from generations ago. And there will be pieces of your love for generations to come that play out in joy, confidence, and bravery. Love may not be the same as power, and it may not always lead to survival, but love, unlike anything, finds a way to live on."

Instead of closing out these liminal spaces—these ghosts of our loved ones—we'd do well to let them in. Like those old Irish folks would do on the last day of October, we can extend hospitality to the ghosts. Ghosts get mad if we shut them out—if we don't acknowledge that love lives on and if we force them into binaries. Repressed emotions, repressed bonds, repressed loved ones can haunt us for the rest of our lives if we decide to shut them out.

This doesn't mean we have to keep all our deceased relatives' stuff and make them scrambled eggs and bacon every morning. But it does mean that closure is a myth. Not only is closure a myth—it's actually harmful, for both the living and the dead.

The dead can be scary if we don't give them space. But if we make peace with our grief, peace with our liminal spaces, and peace with our dead, the ghosts might provide us with favor during the cold, dark winter that lies ahead.

—

A few days after that conversation with Gerda, my phone started making that annoying FaceTime noise that sounds like a combination of an alarm clock and anxiety. It was a FaceTime call from Gerda. Despite that awful ring, Face-Time was a godsend for all those in medical facilities that welcomed few visitors, if any at all, during the pandemic. Like so many others during the pandemic, Gerda was dying alone, save for her FaceTime calls.

"I'm almost dead, so I thought I'd call you one last time to give you an update on whether or not I've caved in to God," Gerda said. Dying was apparently not disrupting her sarcasm.

"The update is that I'm a few days away from death and I'm still an atheist," she told me.

"Well, I'm glad you haven't succumbed to all the religious peer pressure," I told her.

She was lying down on her bed with her phone positioned so that all I could see was her chin. I could tell the yellowish bilirubin was starting to show on her skin. It wasn't long, but she still had the energy to speak her mind.

"I've been seeing Noshi," she said somewhat sheepishly. "My beliefs in God haven't changed, but I'm feeling an innate sense that Noshi is close to me. I still don't know if it's objectively true—that Noshi really is close to me. But this whole dying thing has made my mind feel … well, loose once again."

"Loose!" I exclaimed. "Exactly. That's a great word. And I know what you mean, even though I'm not … well, dying. I think being around death has made my beliefs feel loose, too. Anyway, I interrupted you. You were about to explain how you've been seeing dead people."

"Yes, you did. And yes, I was. I was about to open up to you about something deeply intimate and vulnerable, and you interrupted," she said, with a crooked grin.

"I've been dreaming of Noshi off and on for the past couple of months. You know how dreams often have this feeling that they're in the past, that they're being sourced from prior experiences and just rearranged to have a sense of originality? These dreams are different. They don't feel past, you know? They feel now, alive, and unpredictably original."

"I hardly dream at all," I said. "So yes and no."

She smiled at me. I loved that smile because it usually preceded a witty comeback. This time, however, it didn't.

"When I wake up, I feel less alive, less genuine than I do in my dreams. This here—my conversation with you—feels dreamy. But my dreams, my interactions with Noshi, my conversations with him, all of it seems centered, grounded, and warm. I know it's partially my brain responding to sickness. I know that these low-dosage painkillers are messing with my brain chemistry. I also know that it's not real. But it *is* … real."

Gerda paused to reflect. "I readily admit that I want my husband here with me now. I want to replace my skepticism with the comfort of hope. And I readily admit that this is entirely subjective. It's *not* real, but it *is*."

I nodded.

"Caleb. I'm still an atheist. But I think I can conceive of God and an afterlife."

"Okay ...," I responded with an inquisitive tone.

"You know how I saw Noshi's parents when he died? And you know how that young man saw his dad's death scene with the *Playboy*?"

"Yes. Both of them are mysterious experiences, no?"

"I think I understand them a little, and I think they help me understand how God could exist."

Gerda continued after she had organized her thoughts. "First, I agree with Isaac Newton when he said that 'what we know is a drop, what we don't know is an ocean.' Because there's so much that I don't know, I'm no longer dismissing my experience and the experiences of others with their dead. Instead of calling them stupid 'absurdities' or 'delusions' because I don't understand them, I'm going to call them a 'mystery.'"

"That perspective makes life a little more interesting," I responded.

"It also makes *death* more interesting," she said with a chuckle.

"Second," she said, "I don't believe in the Cartesian view of the soul. Neuroscience shows little evidence that God drops a soul into a body and that the soul is somehow eternal and will last forever, even after the body dies."

"We've talked about this," I replied. "We're on the same page here. I'm not a dualist either."

Gerda continued. "I don't think we're just a bag of chemicals, and neither are we just a soul in a flesh suit. We start with flesh and become a soul, instead of the other way around. This is why I haven't believed in the afterlife. If humans arise from flesh, our demise will coincide with the time when our flesh dies."

I rejoined, "Which is part of the reason why early Christians—borrowing from their Jewish roots—believed in the resurrection of the body instead of the dualism that many of us in the West believe today. And I like that perspective. I like the intrinsic integration between body and soul—and it keeps us accountable too. Because if souls are bodies and bodies are souls, it helps us love our bodies a little more."

"Here's my third thing, Caleb," she said. "Even though the self or soul or body-mind or whatever we want to call it— whatever it is that makes me *me*—it's not limited to our body. This is kind of the theme of many of our conversations. You aren't just you, and I'm not just me."

"And just to let you know," I interjected, "I'm so thankful for you. I'm thankful for your vulnerability. I'm thankful that you let me become a part of you and you become a part of me."

"There isn't one soulmate, Caleb," she said. "Don't ever believe that lie. We'll have many throughout our lifetimes, and you are one of mine."

Gerda said she had one last question for me. I braced myself, although knowing Gerda, I knew her question might hold within itself its own answer. "Let's say I'm wrong about the existence of God," she said. "Let's say there *is* a God. Let's say that God is all-loving, just as you believe. I'd like to think that our afterlife would be in God. Just as I am connected to those I love, if this God loves me, that God would know me so well—be so intimately acquainted with me—that even after my mind-body dies, I could still exist in God-self. Does that make sense?"

I nodded, and she went on. "And Caleb, if all these things are true and real, God's love for me and for the world might be so inextricably connected that I—that *we*—are a part of God. I don't think that means I'd *be* God, although it might. God's love for us is how we exist after life. That love is the foundation for your Christian afterlife."

Gerda paused, and I took the opportunity to cut her off before she went down another thought path. "So let me get this straight. Right now I'm talking to an atheist on her deathbed—and she's explaining the afterlife better than I can?"

"Seems that way," Gerda laughed.

We talked a little bit more about her funeral arrangements, how she wanted to be buried at Green Meadows and have Celeste perform the graveside service. Then we hung up.

—

Ten days later, I was at the front entrance of Hickory House awaiting the nurse to come and take my temperature to make sure I was virus-free before I entered. Gerda was waiting for me in her room. She was dead.

A few skilled nursing facilities in our area were slow adapters to the pandemic. Staff at one nursing home told me as I entered, "You need a mask, but you don't need gloves." This was still at the beginning of the lockdowns, when there was a shortage of gloves for those of us on the low end of the essential worker pyramid of importance. Our funeral home got close to running out of gloves and masks, but our suppliers worked their asses off to get us essentials. I don't know if the care facility was running low on gloves and didn't want to waste their small supply on normal activities or if they just didn't think the virus was worth worrying about. I kind of think it was the latter. No matter the reason, the result was tragic, as they ended up losing one-third of their residents to the coronavirus.

Gerda died about a month into the pandemic, and at that point, most of us knew how dangerous the coronavirus was when it entered a care facility. After the woman at the front desk scanned my forehead, she had me put on gloves, followed by a gown, followed by a plastic face shield. Off we went to get Gerda.

This trip was one of many I had made to care facilities during the pandemic, and each one had the same vibe of loneliness and sadness. I need to say here that the staff who work at skilled nursing facilities worked tirelessly throughout the pandemic. So many lives were lost at nursing homes, and so many of the staff who had developed good relationships with the residents were left to grieve many times over. This affected them physically, and it affected them emotionally. If you get a chance and you find a willing recipient, hug a nurse or health-care worker and tell them thanks.

Walking through the halls of care facilities is often a sad experience. So many lonely eyes peer at you through their rooms, begging for a listening ear and a conversation.

Nurses acknowledge them, but they can only do so much. During the pandemic, walking through the halls of skilled care facilities bore an extra amount of sadness. Not only were the residents alone, barred from the outside world, but many of them were dying alone, uncomforted by the physical presence of those they love.

Gerda died alone. Like so many who died during the pandemic—whether of the virus or something else, whether in hospitals or nursing homes—she died without loved ones by her side. It's horribly sad to contemplate.

After I transferred her over to my stretcher, her mouth open and her body frail, I told her that I was sorry she was alone. I told her that I wish I could have visited.

I solemnly brought her outside to the funeral home's removal van. I loaded her and the stretcher in the back of the van, closed the door, and got in the driver's seat. Then I turned on some Beethoven so she had something comforting on the way back to the funeral home.

———

A few days later, Celeste and I drove together in the hearse up to the Green Meadows Cemetery. At this point, we had both recently been tested for COVID and both of the tests came back negative, so we thought we could safely drive an hour and a half together up to Gerda's gravesite. We talked about everything that was going on in the world, with me mostly listening to her profound thoughts on everything current in the world. I wanted to listen to her and hear her as best I could.

We arrived at Green Meadows to find some of Gerda's friends waiting for us. Gerda had appointed four pallbearers, me being one of them. We took Gerda out of the hearse in her wicker casket. Once we set Gerda over the open grave, we flanked the side of the casket, with two of us going on one side of the casket and the other two of us on the other. We picked up the large ropes that where underneath her casket, a friend of Gerda's pulled the wood support beams out from under the casket, and we slowly lowered her into the grave and rested her casket on top of the dirt. It was just how she had wanted it.

It was fall, and the leaves had turned their radiant yellows, oranges, and reds. As Celeste was beginning to speak, she told us to look at the leaves falling all around us. She said how much she loves how the colorful array of autumn leaves tells us that sometimes dying can be beautiful. She continued, "But it never occurred to me what happens when the leaves break off the tree."

Extemporaneously, she started talking about how dying is that time from when we've let go of the tree, but we haven't hit the ground yet. She continued that when a leaf disconnects, it no longer just feels the air; it starts to dance with it. The dying person is in-between what we left behind and where we'll eventually land, and while we're in-between, we flow in ways that weren't natural when we were connected to the tree. We felt the air when we were connected. It nourished us in life. But as we fall, as we're dying, we move and dance with that unseen realm. As we fall, we're caught up in the invisible world like never before. And something that we've always felt all along throughout our life—like the air to the leaf—becomes so much more real as it shuffles us off the tree, and for a brief time before we hit the ground, we take to flight.

"Gerda told many of us how it felt as she was dancing with the air during these last few days," Celeste concluded. She smiled. "Now, Gerda told me not to speak about God at her graveside service, and I haven't. But, Gerda, I do hope that you have some time to spend with Noshi."

Celeste said amen and handed some of us shovels. We took turns shoveling the dirt back on top of Gerda's casket, filling up the whole grave after about a half hour of work. We talked about Gerda as we shoveled, and we thanked her that she gave us the opportunity to spend some time in her little piece of heaven.

CHAPTER 14

SELVES ACTUALIZATION

If there's anything I've learned in my years as a funeral director, it's that each of us is a living cemetery. We are each full of dead people. The stories of our ancestors and deceased loved ones live on in our bodies.

It's easy for us to think that death is foreign. It used to be something that happened at home, but now death has been put in the hands of the professionals at hospitals and nursing homes. Rarely have we touched a dead body. Even more rarely have we washed one. Most of what we see is ... well, alive. That one-sided perspective that many of us have ends up skewing our view of just how much death is a part of this world. It skews our view of just how much death is a part of our lives. And we forget just how much death is a part of ourselves.

When we see ourselves as liminal, however, death becomes a part of who I am. When I die, it will not be the occurrence of something foreign. It will be a continuation of who I am. I am a creature who is always in-between the land of the living and the land of the dead. Death is not a stranger to fear or a monster that strikes horror in my heart. Death has been a part of me my entire life: from the food I've eaten, to the clothing I've worn, to the ground I walk on, to the DNA that survives from the numerous generations before me.

Most of us like binaries, such as right or wrong, on or off, dead or alive, and the best binary of all: you or me. The sibling of "you or me" is "us or them." But we are all both: "I and you" and "us and them." Stay with me here: if much of the "you" are your ancestors, then much of the "you" isn't "alive." Since I am "I" *and* "you," I am also alive and dead. I sit in the liminality of life and death, just like you do.

Part of accepting ourselves is accepting our liminality. In life we are mortal, and the life that we live is built on a mountain of death. We are made up of the dead and the living. "We are our ancestors' wildest dreams" is an empowering truth that many Black parents have told their children. In John Krasinski's pandemic show, *Some Good News*, Oprah Winfrey tells twenty-two-year-old National Youth Poet Laureate Amanda Gorman: "The dream that your ancestors held for you, you now carry that dream forward in such a way that you wear the crown they made for you." Isaac Newton said that if he had seen further than others, it was only by "standing on the shoulders of giants."

Liminality says that we do wear a crown, and we do stand on giants, and we are our ancestors' dreams. What we do with that crown—what we do now—is up to us. It's our ancestors and us. Collectivism doesn't just mean we're connected to everyone alive. It means we're connected, through liminality, to those past, present, and future.

I am we and we are I.

My ancestors in the funeral business had made a crown for me, and I wanted to sell the kingdom—or at least do a Prince Harry and leave the royal life. The cumulative trauma of death work—six paternal generations and five maternal generations—all resided in me, the heir apparent. We had all given so much to so many people. Death work is heavy work. It's weighty, full of mysteries we'll never understand.

My ancestors might be upset or mad that I want to leave the funeral business. Some of them might be fearful, because they've built their entire identity around their occupation and standing in the Parkesburg community. The Wildes have carried around death. *I* carry death. And I can't carry it any longer.

We have carried death for long enough, and we have done it in neglect of ourselves. We are ready to be healed. And I began to wonder whether my healing could be the healing of all who had gone before.

—

One ancestor stands out to me as likely the most disappointed in my decision to leave the funeral home: Pop-Pop Wilde.

Like I said earlier, when I started at the funeral home in the early 2000s, Pop-Pop was capable of doing every physical task a funeral director needed to do. He could go on house calls and make removals from the second story of a small house. As time passed, he started to lose his eyesight, and age began to take away his physical strength. He slowly found himself less and less involved in the day-to-day operations of the funeral home.

And I was still his right hand. My job at the funeral home became twofold: enabling Pop-Pop to keep doing the cosmetology and dressing of bodies by doing all the physical work he couldn't do, and doing anything around the funeral home that crossed his mind but that was too physically demanding for him. It started to feel like I was working two jobs. As time passed and my own family grew to four, I slowly transitioned away from being Pop-Pop's right hand and into simply doing some parts of his job. It was tough on our relationship, and I'm sorry to say that one of our last conversations was an argument.

On December 16, Pop-Pop drove to Dunkin' Donuts to get his coffee and donut. When he returned home, he walked up his front steps to his house, lost his balance, and fell backward, hitting his back and fracturing some ribs. He was rushed to the hospital. The first brain scan made it seem like the fall had only harmed his back, not his brain.

In the middle of the night, though, I received a call from my mom. She and Dad were driving through a snowstorm to the hospital to say goodbye to Pop-Pop.

"This is it," she said. "He's lost consciousness from a brain bleed, and we want to be there when they take him off the machines."

Knowing that I couldn't go because of the COVID regulations at the hospital, I asked Mom to tell him that I love him and that I'd miss him.

I woke Nicki up and let her know what was happening. She held me in bed, and I eventually fell asleep in her arms.

Pop-Pop died early the next day, December 17, at age eighty-nine, in the middle of a snowstorm.

—

When the sun came up, I jumped in the snowplow and plowed out the funeral home and many of the parking spots on the street, just like usual. But the whole street felt different.

Pop-Pop had lived in the funeral home for most of his life. After Mom-Mom Wilde, my grandma, died in 1992, he eventually got married to Sue, who I've called Nana since I was twelve years old. He bought the house directly across from the funeral home, which is where he and Sue lived for the last twenty-plus years of his life.

As Pop-Pop's physical health had slowly worsened over the course of a few years, he began spending most of his time watching the funeral home from his front porch across the street. When I'd go over to chat with him, he'd want to know everything that was going on at the funeral home and was never afraid to offer his pointed commentary on how we were running the business.

After plowing out the funeral home, I loaded up our removal van and drove through the still snow-covered roads to Lancaster General Hospital, where his body lay waiting for me.

On my way there and back, I didn't feel grief. I wanted to feel sad. I loved my grandfather, and I knew he loved me. But on that day and many days after, I felt mad. I was mad that he had become contentious toward me, that one of our last conversations was an argument. "That's not the way it was supposed to be!" I'd say to him if I could. "Pop-Pop, you and I had nearly twenty years of working side-by-side as a pretty good team up until a few months before your death. We were supposed to end on a high note: me being able to tell you that I love you and you saying the same back to me. That would have been all I needed, and that would have been all you needed."

To this day, I am glad that I never said anything to him that I now regret. I was attempting to guide the funeral home through a pandemic, and I was doing the best I could. Given his increasing limitations and frustration at not being able to do the work he loved, I know he was doing his best too.

—

When Pop-Pop died, our grandson–grandfather relationship wasn't at its best. We had had such a wonderful relationship all the way up to the last couple months before he died. After his death, I felt like I knew he loved me, and that despite some arguments, he was still proud of me. I didn't come to that conclusion lightly. It's a perspective I've grown to understand as I've attempted to speak to Pop-Pop after his death.

If you read my bio before you read the book, you'll know I have two masters degrees, one that focused on theology and another that focused on death in the context of religion and culture. I worked through these programs while working at the funeral home because I genuinely enjoy theology. I'm an Enneagram 4, wing 5, for those of you who are interested, and I want my mind to help guide me through this deep mystery I see all around me and in me. The best way that I can explain my approach to ancestors is to take a super wide-angle lens and look at how a Christian perspective of humanity affects how we approach our ancestors. If you're like "nah" to

Christian theology, I get it. It's too often practiced by white men who believe they know more about life than you do.

But the purpose of theology isn't so people can feel superior. It's meant to make us humble as we examine the mystery of what many people call God.

As science advances, God is getting new names, such as "the Universe" or even "Quantum Mechanics." Because in some way, those psychological and scientific endeavors ask questions that have some shared interest with theology: What is this all about? The Jesus story points toward something called "resurrection," which is why I, as a theologian, believe I can speak to the dead. Trauma produces endless cycles of pain and death, but love gives new life, enabling even the dead to rise into this present moment.

The common belief of many Christians in the United States and the western hemisphere is that sin leads to death. It's based off that popular scripture verse in Romans 6:23: the wages of sin is death. In other words, the reason there's death in the world is because Adam and Eve sinned and were forbidden to eat of the Tree of Life.

In the United States, that scripture verse is often immediately followed by the verse that states all have sinned and fallen short of God's glory. From that verse and others, some Christians believe that humans have a sinful nature that causes them to do sinful acts. Original sin is another negative interpretation of humanity. The Protestant idea of total depravity takes it a step further by saying that we can do nothing right apart from God, that humans are inherently depraved.

These views of human nature have messed up a lot of people by telling them that they are, by default, broken, and never enough. These views say, "Since you're never enough, when you die, you will go directly to hell for being something you never chose to be. You will be punished by God because you've offended God's glory. And you will spend eternity there for what you did in the span of seventy-five years."

Some of you reading this may come from a Christian background that used shame and guilt and hell as control mechanisms. It's true that Christianity is all about repentance and consecration. (I like to define repentance as continuously finding the self-reflective strength to walk on better paths and consecration as the ability to see the sacred in all things.) But it's not about guilt and shame, because I don't think God makes junk. Have you looked at this world? It's unmistakable that the universe we live in is full of wild, mysterious wonder, and there's no reason to believe humans are the exception.

Eastern Orthodox Christianity, in contrast to Western Christianity, takes its cues from another scripture verse that says, "The sting of death is sin" (1 Corinthians 15:56). In other words, from the beginning of our species, our struggle is over how we face death. When death is faced with fear and ignorance, it seems to result in people practicing self-justification and selfishness, resulting in trauma and what is known as "sin" in religious circles. In this view, it's not sin that produces death, it's death that produces sin.

The resurrection of Christ, as viewed by those in the Eastern Orthodox tradition, affirms continuous life and gives humanity hope in the face of death. The idea is that when the power of death is defeated, it ushers in a world that is free of fear and selfishness. The world changes: from survival of the fittest to the care for the hurt and abused. For Eastern Orthodoxy, when humanity commits to the resurrection of the dead, we can reach the next evolutionary step of humanity through something called *theosis*: a transformative process that leads toward union with God, similar to the thoughts Gerda shared about a Christian afterlife.

When I think about ancestors, I envision them in this process of theosis, in which they've become like God by leaving fear behind for love. I view ancestors as beings that can continuously remind us of the value of this present moment that we inhabit right now. They can remind us who we are, as we remember what they've worked for to get us in this moment. They can help us become good ancestors for our descendants and give us visions to bless a thousand generations.

As I've said, our choices today are our children's inheritance tomorrow. We know this because our ancestors have done this for us. They can act as lighthouses because we know that they once sailed in those very same seas and they succeeded to become a guiding light of direction. I'm not encouraging us to see our ancestors in such a positive light because I worship my ancestors or believe they'll bless me by micromanaging my daily affairs. No. I'm telling you that they are here to empower us to become better if we allow them to have space in our lives. They're free from the trauma of this world, and they stand to guide us toward a better humanity. They are part of the resurrection in that they can be voices unfettered by fear of death.

I can remember sitting in the back of Our Lady of Consolation Catholic Church during Joan's funeral on the eve
of Christmas. At that time, I don't think I realized that the
power of love extends beyond this life. I could only see fear
after death. I could only see the afterlife as a product of our
very human fears, guilt, and self-preservation.

In Father Mick's dream, however, Joan arrived to heaven
with a gift. In a departure from most of the heaven stories
I've heard during funerals over the years, Father Mick's
retelling made no mention of mansions, streets of gold,
or rewards. Joan was there to *present* a gift to Jesus, not to
receive one. That gift was us: all the connection and meaning
Joan had invested into us. The gift was her friends and her
family. All the love she had shown in her lifetime had been
wrapped up and presented to God during the Christmas season. This afterlife—Joan's afterlife—wasn't made out of fear
or self-preservation. It was made out of love.

As I've thought about Father Mick's dream over the past
couple of years, something has softly touched the callouses
that had developed from years of handling death. Death can
do that to a person. The painfulness and capricious nature of
death can make the world feel like a cosmic joke, especially
to those of us in the funeral business. It can harden a person
to all that's good.

And then comes love. Love is the Big Bang of meaning.
There's nothing, and then there's something. Something real
that keeps expanding, like the resurrection. Love sits at the
center of all that exists. I don't think there's anything magical
or mysterious about love. Love is the ability to see value in
the other and to create the vulnerable acts of marrying our

value to theirs. To see them as person and not as object. In the framework of German theologian Martin Buber, it's the "I-Thou" instead of the "I-It": seeing connection with others as the end in itself instead of seeing others as a means to an end. Perhaps the saddest people on earth are the ones who can't see love.

Sitting in the pew at Joan's funeral, I was one of those sad people. For multiple reasons, I was sad. I wasn't yet able to see love surviving into the afterlife. Promises of eternal life and eternal rewards seemed to appeal to everything contrary to love. The view of death and the afterlife that I'd heard spoken of in countless sermons seemed to speak of self-interest and wishful thinking.

This life is it, perhaps. Perhaps not. I'm not sure we can know entirely at this chapter in humanity's understanding of the universe. What we do know is that we don't just embody ourselves. As a living cemetery, we embody our ancestors. As a living womb, we embody our descendants.

Trauma can live on and repeat itself in cycles, but it's love that breaks the cycle and moves onward forever, like the Big Bang. Maybe the Big Bang of meaning can create something from the nothing of death.

Maybe love can even cross the boundaries of life and death. In fact, it can. It can cross those boundaries. And when we believe that our ancestors have seen that love and entered theosis, they become approachable.

Our ancestors aren't wrapped in the fear that they once were. They are wrapped in the resurrection.

—

Six months after his death, I decided it was time to talk to Pop-Pop. I had been doing some talking with some of my ancestors, thanks to Peggy's suggestion. The idea of talking to the dead—not to mention listening to what they have to say—still strikes me as a bit strange, and I wouldn't be surprised if it strikes you that way too.

These conversations, though, aren't like a conversation you and I would have. I suppose this could be called ancestral meditation. To have these conversations, I have to be in a certain state of mind. If my mind is distracted, I don't feel like I can listen well.

For me to have this type of conversation, I have to both focus on my ancestors and give my mind permission to lay aside skepticism and doubt. I have to just listen. I don't want to say that it's an anti-intellectual process, but I do have to quiet the loudest voices in my head, including the skeptic inside of me. I tell my inner skeptic that I'll listen to their voice after this conversation is over, but that for now, I'm going to enter into a different space. In this space, I listen for other voices—voices I often tell to be quiet simply because I don't believe them to be real.

In fact, whether something is "real" or "not real" is not the rubric I use anymore to judge the conversations I have with my ancestors. The rubric isn't judgment at all, at least when I'm in conversation. The rubric is listening.

During high school, I prayed and meditated about two hours a day. As I mentioned earlier, my commitment to prayer and meditation had my parents occasionally calling me a monk. Over my high school years, I learned to quiet my mind and listen. I learned to go into a space that feels timeless. There's no realization of the clock, no realization of external surroundings, just an overwhelming sense of centering in your present being. For a writer, I'm not doing a very good job explaining it. But if you've experienced this space, you know it.

Even though I don't practice meditation and prayer like I did in high school, I can still find this meditative space. My surroundings have to be quiet—and not just quiet in the noise department, but quiet in the sense of an absence of demands, obligations, and to-do lists. The one space I've found where I can quiet all the voices is in my shower. Nearly every morning, I sit in the confines of my shower, where I can't hear any outside noise, and I find that space. I allow those demands, obligations, and to-do lists to shrink to the background, and I allow my mind to turn off. It's easy to lose track of time, and I have to set an alarm to go off after a certain amount of time. But even then, it's hard for me to disengage from mediation, and it's made me late to work on more than one occasion.

At this time in my life, the quietest place is Peggy's little therapy office. Peggy's friendship and her affirmation in my life has just made her office feel like home. Every time I go to therapy, I'm attacked with kisses from the dogs as soon as I open the sliding glass door and sit down on the couch. They snuggle me, and Dexter, especially, loves lying beside me when I'm doing some of the meditative work.

In her therapy office, I ignore my cell phone, I don't hear my kids at each other's throats, and I've put fifteen miles between me and the funeral home. Aside from Peggy's quiet presence, there's no one demanding my attention. I'll lie on the office sofa and cover myself from head to toe with a weighted blanket. In the quiet, I allow my mind to start listening for voices.

Today I picture myself on Pop-Pop's front porch, where so much of his recent judgment has been expressed to me. Biting judgment, even: not the kind your uncle gives you after he's put a few down, but the kind that's pointed at weaknesses only a loved one would know.

I understand Pop-Pop wasn't healthy. How hard it must have been for him to be at the top of his game only ten years earlier and then—during a time when the funeral home needed help—be relegated to the sidelines of his front porch. I know it will be hard for me to accept my own physical failings as I age. I'm probably going to be the eighty-five-year-old who's up on a ladder trying to clean his gutters. Pop-Pop was frustrated by his decline and inability to run the funeral home like he once could. He was sitting on the bench, but he still saw himself as the starting quarterback. I get that.

As Pop-Pop and I sit on that front porch in the space of my ancestral meditation, it is quiet at first, with neither one of us initiating conversation. I feel a strong sense that he knows that I have been angry at him. Perhaps, now that he is no longer held by the mortal coil, he can see my good intentions.

"How's Mom-Mom doing?" I ask him.

"Good," he says, as he crosses his legs, folds his hands over his top knee, and leans back against the wall. "It is so good to see her. Caleb, she's proud of you."

A moment passes, and he continues. "I'm sorry for the last couple of months, Caleb. I saw your strengths and I wanted them here at the funeral home. I wanted to protect you. It's safe here at this business, you know. It's a steady income, and you get to do rewarding work at the same time. I know you're strong enough to do something outside the funeral home. I don't understand why you can't stay, but I do accept it."

Another silent moment passes between us, and then I ask him why he didn't tell me these things when he was alive. Why didn't he tell me that I could leave if I wanted to?

"I was afraid, Calebee, that the funeral home would fall apart without you. That there wouldn't be a sixth-generation Wilde to carry on the business."

He uncrosses his legs and leans forward. "I'm not afraid of that now. I can see that the funeral home has always just been a by-product of our family's love, creativity, and work ethic. Those core values are what matter to me now. If you take those core values wherever you go, you'll be continuing our legacy. As much as I want the legacy to continue through the funeral home, as long as you love wherever you go, we'll be with you." Pop-Pop had difficulty communicating his feelings during his life, because such things weren't taught to boys of his generation. But he often said "I love you" before he ended a phone conversation. His "I love yous" weren't cheap ones. They held real value.

"That's what I want, now, Calebee. I just want to come with you guys." He leans over to give me a hug, which is what I think I really want. The hug is such a clear communicator, especially between a grandfather and his grandson. You don't have to interpret and extrapolate from a grandfather's hug. You just know it's love.

"One last thing," he says, as he speaks in his quiet voice that he'd so often use at arrangements. "Gerda didn't die alone.

Her loved ones were with her. I thought you should know. Nobody dies alone, Calebee. Nobody."

Usually, when we picture a spirit or a ghost, they vanish into thin air, like mist being hit by the sun. As our conversation ends, Pop-Pop begins to vanish. But he doesn't vanish into thin air. He vanishes into me. It's as if I am now carrying him, just as he has carried me.

It's true for all of us: for my parents, my grandparents, Joan's family, Diane's husband and kids, Dwayne's two daughters, and J. J. and his grandma Patricia, Gerda, and Celeste. Their loved ones are still alive in them. Of course our dead are still speaking.

We carry them in us.

EPILOGUE

You might be wondering what I'm going to do if I leave the funeral home. It's a good question, one that currently doesn't have an exact answer. Even though I've committed to leave the funeral home now, I don't know what the future will bring. If I've learned anything from working with death it's that we can't predict as much as we think we can. Perhaps I just need a sabbatical.

But right now, as I write this in my office, I have just met with three families over the past few days, all of whom had lost their loved ones to COVID. I need to know myself away from the funeral home. Find out who I am when I'm not dealing with death.

What I'm planning to do is a dream I've had since I was a teenager: I love thinking about God. The same questions in my mind are being asked by so many scientists, social justice leaders, psychologists, neurobiologists, and people who work their tails off paying the man on a nine-to-five, earning just above minimum wage—and I can't wait to learn more from all of them. I'd love to help people who have been hit the hardest by fearing death in all the wrong ways. Trauma. PTSD. Injustice. I want to do theology for the people who need the hope of the resurrection. That's what I'm going to do.

I'm crying as I write this. It's been so long since I've cried, because I've become hard to the world, you know? It's been a hard two decades for me. Really hard. I have felt so many people's pain. I've also felt rejected by God, if I'm honest. It has felt so lonely at the funeral home. So sad. And so hard with personal family dynamics that created friction in an already tense work environment. Now, for some reason, I feel like it's time to the leave the funeral home and take the heart that I've been given by others and do my part to do something that gives life. I want to give life. Can you blame me? Death is so dark. I don't know how so many funeral directors have done it for fifty years. Twenty years in the industry has been more than enough for me. It's time for me to take what I've learned and bring a little life to the death that's literally haunted my professional life and occupation.

At the beginning of this book, I talked about how I had started to believe that eternal life and thoughts of heaven were just a coping mechanism for the insurmountable darkness of death. I don't believe that anymore. I believe that love can create resurrection, the hope that there's more to come, however that may look.

I love you all. Thanks for reading my book. My hope is that you find empowerment from your dead by bringing them into your life. That's exactly what I'm going to do too.

ACKNOWLEDGMENTS

The people who deserve the most thanks are the ones who have sacrificed the most for this book: Nicki, Jeremiah, and Demarco. When I signed this book contract at the start of the pandemic, I made it my purpose to prioritize and surround you all with my love. Still, there were many nights when this book project took me away from you, perhaps during times that you needed me close. I know what you've sacrificed, and I promise I'm doing the best I know how to bring more love into our lives. To Valerie: thank you for striking the difficult balance of being gentle, patient, and understanding with me as I wrote this manuscript while also holding my writing accountable to high editorial standards. To Peggy: thanks for being my mentor, friend, and therapist, and for guiding me through the last few years of a difficult journey, a journey that's become a book. To Matthew Paul Turner, for your constant encouragement, love, banter, and of course the wonderful photos you manage to take of my face. To Rob Bell, for planting the seeds that grew to this. To Jackie Moriniere, for helping me create a more accurate representation of Celeste. To Evan and Davey, for being good friends. To SFB, you know who you are and you know I love you all, even though I've been largely absent in everyone's lives over this past year and a half. And lastly, to my dad (your kindness and compassion is all throughout my writing) and my mom (the passion you have for the people you love is all throughout my writing), my grandparents, and all the spoken and unspoken ancestors who have made me who I am. I promise you all: you're coming with me.

NOTES

Preface

xiii   *One study that analyzed:* Tatsuya Morita et al., "Nationwide Japanese Survey About Deathbed Visions: 'My Deceased Mother Took Me to Heaven'," *Journal of Pain and Symptom Management* 52, no. 5 (2016): 646–654.e5.

Chapter 1

9   *"Death, like the sun":* François de la Rochefoucauld. Reflections; or Sentences and Moral Maxims. https://www.jstor.org/stable/25660701.

10   *To reinforce belief in heaven:* Sheldon Solomon, Jeff Greenberg, and Tom Pyszczynski, "The Cultural Animal: Twenty Years of Terror Management Theory and Research," in *Handbook of Experimental Existential Psychology,* eds. J. Greenbert, S. L. Koole, and T. Pyszczynski (New York: Guilford Press, 2004), 20.

11   *"Vigorous agreement with":* Solomon et al., "The Cultural Animal," 20–21.

Chapter 6

70   *Here is the tale of the event:* I'm indebted to the following sources for my retelling of the account of the Christiana Resistance in this chapter:

David R. Forbes, *A True Story of the Christiana Riot* (Quarryville, PA: The Sun Printing House, 1898); Jonathan Katz, *Resistance at Christiana* (New York: Thomas Y. Crowell, 1974); and L. D. Rettew, *Treason at Christiana: September 11, 1851* (Morgantown, PA: Masthof Press, 2006).

Chapter 7

89   *"Spiritual crisis in white America"*: Ruby Sales, Interview with Krista Tippett, "Where Does It Hurt?" *On Being*, National Public Radio, September 15, 2016.

93   *"One who is supporting"*: Ibram X. Kendi, *How to Be An Antiracist* (New York: One World, 2019), 13.

Chapter 10

130   *"There are twenty thousand tons"*: Mark Harris, *Grave Matters: A Journey Through the Modern Funeral Industry to a Natural Way of Burial* (New York: Scribner, 2008).

Chapter 12

164   *"Some things in life"*: Megan Devine, *"It's OK That You're Not OK: Meeting Grief and Loss in a Culture That Doesn't Understand* (Boulder, CO: Sounds True, 2017), 3.

Chapter 14

188   *"The dream that your ancestors held"*: SomeGoodNews, "SGN Graduation with Oprah, Steven Spielberg, Jon Stewart, and Malala (Ep. 6)," May 3, 2020, YouTube video, 21:00, https://www.youtube.com/watch?v=IweS2CPSnbI.